"GO TAKE IT BACK! –
RECLAIMING HOPE AFTER DESPAIR"

Dr Phillip J. O'Connor

PROFESSIONAL SPEAKING SERVICES

Theme and Scripture References

> And David inquired of the LORD, "Shall I pursue this raiding party? Will I overtake them?" "Pursue them," He answered. "You will certainly overtake them and succeed in the rescue." (1 Samuel 30:8, NIV)
>
> And I will restore to you the years that the locust hath eaten, the cankerworm, and the caterpillar, and the palmerworm, my great army which I sent among you. (Joel 2:25 KJV)

Dr Phillip J. O'Connor

University lecturer, Teacher, International Conference, Inspirational & Itinerant Speaker; Author, Broadcaster, Youth Minister, Musician, Academic and Life Mentor.

About The Author

Dr Phillip J. O'Connor is a passionate teacher, Sessional Academic lecturer, Inspirational and itinerant speaker dedicated to inspiring transformation. With four decades of teaching experience across Jamaica, the Cayman Islands, and the UK, he has trained and mentored students, educators, and leaders.

From a young age, Phillip embraced faith; preaching, singing in various choirs, and playing guitar in the University Singers and a number of Gospel Bands. His ministry took him to the Cayman Islands, where he served as a full-time Youth Minister for three years in Bodden Town, and teacher at the Creative Christian Character (Triple C) school for 6 years. He also led a dynamic 4-hour weekly radio program 'Times of Refreshing' on ICCI-FM 101.1 from 1996-2001 and empowered young people to live with purpose.

A British citizen by birth, he returned to England in 2001 and continued his mission in Education and speaking in various locations in Kent, Dalston, Tottenham, Blackheath, Bromley, Northolt, Gloucester, Bedford, Wales plus online Networks (USA and Jamaica). Phillip also presented academic papers at international conferences in University of Oslo, Norway; Dublin, Liverpool Hope University and Canterbury Christ Church University.

Armed with a Doctorate in Education and a passion for change, Dr O'Connor speaks to various audiences on personal growth, faith, leadership, and mindset shifts, challenging individuals to reclaim hope and step into their purpose. Now semi-retired, he continues to inspire audiences across the UK, USA, Cayman Islands, Jamaica and wider afield primarily through his YouTube Channel: https://www.youtube.com/@drphillipjoconnor3848/videos.

He is the author of *'Safely Through on Broken Pieces – Focus on What You Have Left, Not on What You Have Lost'* and Chapter 5 in *'Being Christian in Education.'*

He is married to Rhona O'Connor, a dedicated registered nurse, and both are foster carers.

Listening To Your Voice Publishing

Empowering Transformations   www.ltyvpublishing.co.uk

Dedication and Acknowledgements

—————— 99 ——————

To the memory of the late Mrs. Dunkley; teachers, university lecturers, professors and the incredible community of faith and friends who have mentored, supported, and walked beside me from childhood to this moment. Your prayers, wisdom, and encouragement have helped shaped my journey.

To my wife, Rhona, and our family, your love, strength, and unwavering faith have been my anchor. To my dear mother, Mrs. Thelma O'Connor and father, the late Mr Lamech O'Connor, who nurtured me in faith and resilience; and my cherished siblings (Lonnie, Ronnie, Sharon, Brenda, Collin, Barrington and Sylvia); I am forever grateful.

With heartfelt gratitude and appreciation, I thank you all. Your steadfast love reflects God's promise: *"I will restore to you the years that the locust hath eaten"* (Joel 2:25).

May this book be a testament to the power of faith, hope, and reclaiming what was lost. The topic of my previous book sums it up very well: '*Safely Through on Broken Pieces – Focus on what you have left, not on what you have lost.*'

With deepest thanks,

Phillip

Contents

Foreword

———————— 99 ————————

Relevant, revolutionary, and saturated with the essence of transformational power, *Go Take It Back! Reclaiming Hope After Despair* is a timely and transformative contribution to the discourse on psychological resilience, spiritual restoration, and human flourishing. Dr. Phillip O'Connor presents a narrative of recovery and a compelling framework for personal renewal through adversity.

As a Counselling Psychologist, I am deeply aware of how despair often distorts perception, diminishes agency, and threatens the self's capacity for hope. Yet in these very crucibles, Dr. O'Connor uncovers the possibility of reclamation, courage forged through vulnerability and strength discovered in surrender and resilience.

Drawing on David's account at Ziklag, as well as his own personal experiences, he challenges the reader to develop a Christ-like mindset; one that acknowledges, confronts, and transcends fear and resists paralysis. This mindset persists through despair by clinging to hope and purposefully and prayerfully pursuing and reclaiming what was lost.

This is more than inspiration. It is an invitation. If you find yourself overwhelmed by life's trials or uncertain about navigating the aftermath of profound loss or disillusionment, this book is for you. It is both a practical and spiritual map for those who are ready not just to survive, but to live again and thrive with purpose, conviction, and hope.

Dr. O'Connor dares us to confront our despair, not to deny it, but to reclaim what it tried to take. In these pages, you will find challenge, yes, but also profound encouragement. The journey is not easy, but it is possible, and for those willing to embrace the process, healing is not just a hope but a promise.

Mr Kevin Bailey BA, MA (Counselling Psychology)

Licensed Associate Counselling Psychologist

Co-Host: The Male Box, Love FM 101.1 – Jamaica

Background

─────────── 99 ───────────

I still vividly remember that sunny Friday afternoon long after school dismissal as if it were yesterday. As Head Boy or School Captain of my High school, I had just finished drafting the duty rota and assigning approximately forty prefects to various tasks around the school for the following week. These included the main and back gate, canteen, corridor patrol, assembly, form time supervision, and uniform checks. I walked slowly but purposefully through the silent corridors, making my way home after a long and challenging but rewarding week.

Mrs. Dunkley, our warm-hearted Home Economics teacher, was also working late that afternoon. She politely greeted me as our paths crossed. Instead of a casual nod or a brief greeting, she stopped to ask if I was alright and how I was coping with the demands of being Head boy for a school with such large student population. With a mix of hesitation and relief, I confided in her about the demanding schedule of domestic activities that I was juggling alongside my school duties, as the main issues at home that left me feeling tired and overwhelmed.

When my parents and siblings returned to Jamaica from the United Kingdom, we had to carve out a new life from scratch. It was an uphill battle: gruelling farm work under the scorching sun, long hours of labour after school, weekends and holidays that left little time for rest, let alone some of the normal activities of youth.

The relentless demands of domestic responsibilities weighed heavily on me, draining both my body and mind. Balancing school with backbreaking chores was challenging; exhaustion often dulled my focus, and the burden of duty overshadowed my academic work. Yet, amid the struggle, a quiet resilience grew, a determination to reclaim hope from despair.

Mrs Dunkley's response was not one of judgment but of deep care. She suggested I consider seeing the medical doctor, because, 'Of course you are not made out of steel' she said. She suggested specifically the doctor who was also the Chairman of the school board not just to address my physical fatigue, but to hopefully address the unseen wounds caused by a life of extremely hard work on the farm lived too hard, too fast. That simple act of compassion: listening, understanding, and guiding me towards help, became a turning point in my life.

Taking her advice was the first step toward rest and healing. I graciously thanked her and continued my 20-minute walk to the town centre, where I would get the last bus before walking another 40 minutes or so home to the rural village.

I told Mom about our conversation and what Mrs Dunkley had said. I was very concerned because Mom had her Saturdays well planned out as she would usually sell the produce from our farm. This was our main source of income. Nevertheless, without hesitation, she decided to forgo her trip to the market and take me to the doctor the very next day, in Old Harbour, quite a distance away.

The School Board Chairman who was also a Medical doctor was not in office, so we decided to see another doctor who was next door instead of wasting the long and costly trip. He listened to my gruelling schedule and demanding workload on the farm and all my childhood and teenage life activities; planting and watering various crops, looking after the animals, reaping fruits and vegetables, plus chores, to name a few.

Following his examinations, he provided a note advising me to remain at home for a period of two weeks to rest and refrain entirely from engaging in any academic activities. This recommendation represented a significant request, as it coincided with the commencement of my Year 11 GCSE examinations.

With such professional support and my network of family, friends and Saints, I learned to balance my responsibilities and burdens. I discovered that accepting help was not a sign of weakness, but a courageous act of self-care.

I truly appreciate the immense effort and sacrifices my parents made to protect and provide for us. Their hard work and dedication gave me opportunities I will always be grateful for. At the same time, balancing those responsibilities did have an impact on my academic performance. However, I recognise that every challenge I faced has shaped my resilience and work ethic, and I deeply respect the values my parents instilled in me through their own perseverance.

After leaving High school and awarded the prize for Student leadership, I successfully applied for a post at the Jamaica Information Service (JIS) in 1982. I served in the accounting department for six months. Partially inspired by Mrs. Dunkley's kindness, I left after six months and chose a path where I could offer that same compassion to others.

I pursued a career in teaching in September 1982 at the Joint Board of Teacher Education, (Mico Teacher's College), University of the West Indies (now Mico University), driven by a deep-seated desire to create classrooms that were not just centres for academic learning, but sanctuaries where every student felt seen, heard, and supported. I adopted the Motto: '*To care and so to teach*' and later embraced the mantra: '*Motivate, Inspire, Challenge, Encourage and Empower.*'

Over the course of more than 40 years in Education, I've seen the transformative power of empathy first-hand. I have trained teachers, mentored colleagues, supported students through challenging times, and celebrated their successes with the same genuine care that once helped lift me up. Every lesson I teach, every conversation I have, is infused with the spirit of that pivotal moment on the school corridor, a reminder that sometimes, one kind gesture can change the trajectory of a life.

Now, as I reflect on my journey, I am profoundly grateful for that encounter with Mrs. Dunkley. It taught me that true leadership and success are measured not by the burdens we carry, but by the compassion we extend to others along the way.

At the same time, I again also pay tribute to my parents, Mrs. Thelma and the late Mr. Lamech O'Connor, who, despite having only a primary school education, demonstrated remarkable care, resilience, and dedication in raising eight children: five teachers, one Chemist and two nurses; spanning careers in Education, Medicine, Charity, Pharmaceutical, Entrepreneurship and Law.

They instilled in us a strong sense of ambition, aspiration that drives high attainment; and the belief that education is the key or vehicle to upward social mobility, despite facing hardships, struggles, and scarcity. They gave us the best they could with what they knew and had at the time, for which we are truly grateful.

Preface Summary

———————— 99 ————————

Setting the Stage for Transformation and Restoration

This story begins with a vivid, sensory-rich scene, an afternoon steeped in the weight of a challenging school day, mirroring the isolation and exhaustion I carried as a Year 11 student. Through this detailed setting, I hope to immerse you in a moment that not only captures a specific time and place but also echoes the deep struggles I faced; both the visible burdens of responsibility and the challenge of balancing domestic, personal and academic rigour. Yet, even in the midst of weariness, I am reminded of Jesus' words in Matthew 11:28 (NIV): "Come to me, all you who are weary and burdened, and I will give you rest."

Unexpected Intervention

The unexpected encounter with Mrs. Dunkley proved to be a pivotal moment in my journey. Her quiet compassion altered the course of my path. With a simple yet profound question; an inquiry into my well-being, she became the gentle force that nudged me toward self-discovery and healing. Her suggestion to seek professional help was more than mere advice; it was an unexpected but welcomed intervention, illuminating possibilities I had not yet considered.

This account underscores a critical theme; vulnerability is not a weakness. By revealing my personal struggles and accepting help, I demonstrate that acknowledging one's own needs is both courageous and transformative. This narrative, from isolation to seeking and receiving support, serves as a powerful reminder that healing often begins with the willingness to be open and receptive to care.

Transformation Through Experience

My narrative shifts from personal hardships to a journey or process of growth, passion and purpose; a fervent desire to reclaim all that I had lost emotionally, physically and above all, academically. The initial act of kindness not only provided immediate relief but also contributed significantly to my lifelong path in Education.

For over forty years, this journey has been more than just a path; it has been a transformation, shaping me into the person I am today. What once began as personal growth has blossomed into a sacred calling, a profound vocation that allows me to extend the same compassion, guidance, and unwavering support that once uplifted me. Just as I was nurtured in times of need, I now have the privilege of being a vessel of encouragement and hope for others (See Appendix - Subject: Gratitude for Your Impact on My Educational Journey page 200).

This journey reminds me of 2 Corinthians 1:3-4 (NIV)

"Praise be to the God and Father of our Lord Jesus Christ, the Father of compassion and the God of all comfort, who comforts us in all our troubles, so that we can comfort those in any trouble with the comfort we ourselves receive from God."

Through the trials and triumphs of life, I have come to understand that every experience has prepared me for this divine purpose, to be a beacon of light for those walking a similar road. And in doing so, I am reminded that our greatest struggles often lead to our most meaningful callings.

While this narrative primarily emphasises academic restoration, it is important to acknowledge that true restoration is far more nuanced and multifaceted. It encompasses emotional, spiritual, relational, and other dimensions of life. The journey toward wholeness involves confronting and addressing life's challenges in their entirety; not in pursuit of perfection, but as a means of reclaiming hope following seasons of despair, extending beyond the academic realm.

My personal experience serves as a testament to how individual stories can inspire broader, constructive societal impact. Therefore, I encourage others to recognise and value their own narratives. As the saying goes, "Failure is not falling down, but failing to get up." A passage of Scripture that has provided me with profound encouragement during times of restoration is found in Joel 2:25 (NKJV): "So I will restore to you the years that the swarming locust has eaten, the crawling locust, the consuming locust, and the chewing locust, My great army which I sent among you."

You will reclaim all that you have lost, hence, Reclaim hope from the depths of your darkest despair! 'Go, Take it Back!'

Introduction and Inspiration

—————— 99 ——————

Loss is a universal experience. How we respond to it can determine our growth socially, emotionally, spiritually, and personally. In this book, I focus on reclaiming what has been lost, whether in love, relationships, personal aspirations, goals, opportunities, influence, education, finances, or spiritual growth; in essence, reclaiming hope after despair.

Inspired by the story of David at Ziklag in 1 Samuel 30:1-17, and my own story, I will explore overcoming setbacks through faith in God, decisive action and resilience. It includes faith-driven principles, values, leadership approaches, and strategic methods. I will also look at personal qualities and attitudes that help in times of disruption, devastation, discouragement, despair, or disaster.

Although I am writing this book from a faith-based perspective, its principles and strategies are designed to resonate with those of faith and those without. I hope that it will inspire, motivate, challenge, encourage, and empower a broad audience.

In every human life, there comes a moment when the weight of despair seems to shadow every possibility; when the world appears dim and the path ahead, obscured. "*Go Take It Back! Reclaiming Hope After Despair*" originated from personal experiences and was inspired by one of my sermons of the same name. It is both a call to be assertive and a compassionate guide for anyone who has ever felt lost in the depths of hopelessness, urging readers to reclaim whatever was once thought irretrievably lost.

A Journey from Darkness to Light

Imagine standing at the edge of a vast, stormy sea, with waves of uncertainty and despair crashing relentlessly against the shore. In that moment, hope may feel like a distant lighthouse, a mere myth or a distant memory. Yet, the truth is that hope is not an elusive dream; it can be cultivated and reclaimed. I invite you to embark on a journey where despair is acknowledged as a valid and inevitable part of the human condition, but never as a permanent destination.

I will show that even in our darkest hours, the power to transform our inner narrative lies within us. We are reminded in Scripture that '…Greater is He that is in us, than he that is in the world.' (1 John 4:4, KJV). In and of ourselves, we can do nothing, but we are confident that 'The eternal God is our refuge, and underneath are the everlasting arms' (Deuteronomy 33:27, KJV).

The Anatomy of Despair and the Resilience of Hope

Despair often stems from the false belief that our circumstances cannot change. But that is not the truth. I will challenge this mindset, exploring the spiritual, psychological, and emotional roots of hopelessness. Through my personal experiences, real-world examples, and the biblical story of David at Ziklag, we see that despair is not the end; it is a call to rise. With faith in God, prayer, and hope, what feels like defeat can become the turning point for renewal and victory. Scripture reminds us that, "Weeping may endure for a night, but joy comes in the morning" (Psalm 30:5. KJV).

Hope, however, is not merely a passive longing for a better future. Scripture exhorts us, "Hope thou in God: for I shall yet praise Him, who is the health of my countenance, and my God" (Psalm 42:11, KJV). True hope is an active and steadfast trust in the Lord, a deliberate choice to look beyond present trials and embrace the promise of divine restoration. When anchored in God, hope becomes a refuge, a shield against life's burdens, and a catalyst for renewal. In this light, hope is not just an abstract concept but a spiritual discipline, an instrument of transformation, healing, and restoration.

Strategies to Reclaim Hope

The principles and strategies presented in *Go Take It Back!* are both analytical and pragmatic, derived from a thorough examination and deeply informed by my personal experiences. As mentioned, these insights are also inspired by David and his followers, as recorded in 1 Samuel 30, who transformed their adversity into a catalyst for resilience and triumph. This narrative is not a straightforward account; rather, it encapsulates a complex journey, as exemplified by David's experiences at Ziglag. His story traverses a continuum from hope to disappointment, discouragement, despondency, devastation, disaster, and destitution, ultimately culminating in the restoration of hope, deliverance and victory.

Here are a few key themes I will explore in this book:

- **Reclaiming Agency:** When the storms of life seem overwhelming, remember that "God has not given us a spirit of fear, but of power, and of love, and of a sound mind" (2 Timothy 1:7, NKJV). Acknowledge the areas where you have been entrusted with stewardship, for "whatever your hand finds to do, do it with all your might" (Ecclesiastes 9:10, NIV). Take small but faithful steps, trusting that "a man plans his way, but the Lord directs his steps" (Proverbs 16:9 NKJV).

- **Rewriting Your Narrative:** "For as a man thinketh in his heart, so is he" (Proverbs 23:7, KJV). The narratives we internalise profoundly shape our perception of reality. Rooted in the transformative wisdom of Scripture, this approach aligns with Romans 12:2 (NIV): "Be transformed by the renewing of your mind."

Additionally, 2 Corinthians 10:5 (NIV) reinforces this pursuit: "We demolish arguments and every pretension that sets itself up against the knowledge of God, and we take captive every thought to make it obedient to Christ." Through intellectual discernment and spiritual renewal, these principles empower us to break free from mental strongholds and embrace a life of faith, purpose, and victory.

- **Renewal of the Mind**: As it is written, "This is the day that the Lord has made; let us rejoice and be glad in it" (Psalm 118:24, ESV). This is more than a pronouncement of mere positive thinking but a declaration of faith based on the Word of God. We are encouraged to trust in God's provision and release the burdens of the past and the worries of the future. Our Lord Jesus instructs us, "Do not worry about tomorrow, for tomorrow will worry about itself. Each day has enough trouble of its own" (Matthew 6:34, NIV).

By setting our minds on what is true and good, as Paul exhorts, "Whatever is true, whatever is noble, whatever is right, whatever is pure, whatever is lovely, whatever is admirable, if anything is excellent or praiseworthy, think about such things" (Philippians 4:8, NIV), we cultivate a heart of gratitude and hope. The renewal of our minds, as described in Romans 12:2 above, allows us to break free from negative thinking and embrace the peace that surpasses all understanding (Philippians 4:7).

Thus, by living in the present and fixing our eyes on Christ, we cast aside the weight of past regrets and future anxieties, making room for hope to flourish in the promises of God.

Community and Connection: "For if they fall, the one will lift up his fellow: but woe to him that is alone when he falleth; for he hath not another to help him up" (Ecclesiastes 4:10, KJV). Verily, despair doth grow in the heart of the one who walketh alone, for in solitude the soul is burdened without solace. But the Lord hath ordained the gathering of brethren, that they may bear one another's burdens and strengthen the weary.

As it is written, "Bear ye one another's burdens, and so fulfil the law of Christ." – Galatians 6:2 (KJV).

Do not walk this journey alone, for even Christ chose to surround Himself with those who uplifted and shared in His mission of love. Seek out positive associations; be it family, steadfast friends, or a community of faith, so that in times of trial or despair, you may find strength, encouragement, and unwavering support. Remember the promise of God stated above: "Two are better than one, because they have a good reward for their labour. For if they fall, one will lift up his companion." (Ecclesiastes 4:9-10, KJV) Let us build each other up, for together, we stand unshaken.

Take heart and build a strong and united community, for wisdom flourishes in shared counsel, and strength is found in unity. When hearts come together in love, hope is reignited, and the darkness of despair fades before the light of true fellowship.

Bridging my Journey with the Call to "Go, Take It Back!"

"Go Take It Back" is more than just a collection of strategies outlined in one of my sermons. It provides principles for reclaiming what you have lost howsoever caused. In its invitation to transform despair into light, I see a reflection of my own personal journey. I challenge the notion that despair is an inevitable part of life, asserting instead that hope is promised through Jesus Christ as we reclaim through prayer, conscious effort and deliberate action what we have lost. Be reminded that no matter how deep the despair, there is always a path back to hope and restoration. As Psalm 34:18 (NIV) reminds us, 'The Lord is close to the broken-hearted and saves those who are crushed in spirit.'

In introducing this book, I invite you to not only read but to engage: to experiment with the strategies, reflect on your own experiences, and join a community of individuals who have decided to reclaim their power. This is your invitation to transform despair into hope, to rewrite your narrative, and ultimately, to take back the promise of a brighter tomorrow.

Let this book be your companion on the journey, your guide in the art of reclaiming hope, and a testament to the resilience that lies within each of us. Go take it back – Reclaim hope over despair!

Reclaiming Hope After Despair

I further invite you to challenge the notion that despair is inevitable, encouraging you to take intentional steps toward hope. Scripture reminds us that "weeping may stay for the night, but rejoicing comes in the morning" (Psalm 30:5, NIV). In my own life, there were times when challenges felt overpowering, yet through total dependence on God and small acts of faith and courage, I discovered that hope was never truly lost, it was waiting to be reclaimed. This reflects the heart of this book's message: no matter how deep the valley, "the light shines in the darkness, and the darkness has not overcome it" (John 1:5, ESV).

Transformation Through Adversity

David's journey from a humble shepherd to a victorious king is a powerful testament to transformation and God's faithfulness. His life, shaped by rejection, divine intervention, and ultimate triumph, reminds us that no setback is final. Just as David faced giants; both literal and figurative, we too will encounter trials that seem overwhelming. Yet, these very challenges can be the stepping stones to our greatest victories.

Your story and mine, like his, are woven with struggles, but also with breakthroughs ordained by God. Every hardship is an opportunity for renewal, and every setback can set the stage for a comeback. As mentioned, Psalm 30:5 (KJV) declares, "Weeping may endure for a night, but joy comes in the morning." And just as God strengthened David, He strengthens us: "The Lord is my strength and my shield; my heart trusts in Him, and He helps me" (Psalm 28:7, NKJV).

Take heart, your transformation is unfolding, and just like David, you are destined for victory!

You Are Not Alone: Finding Strength in Community

If you're feeling lost or overwhelmed, know that you are not alone. *Go Take It Back* is more than just a set of sermon strategies; it's an invitation to reclaim your power alongside others who understand your struggles. My own journey has been transformed by the support and shared experiences of a community that refuses to give up. By opening up about our challenges and victories, we remind each other that hope is never out of reach. Together, we can rewrite our futures and find strength in unity.

Even in our darkest moments, there is hope. As Isaiah 41:10 (NIV) reminds us: "So do not fear, for I am with you; do not be dismayed, for I am your God. I will strengthen you and help you; I will uphold you with my righteous right hand."

Leadership and Self-Discovery

David's rise from a humble shepherd to a mighty king, despite trials and tribulations, stands as a testament to God's power in shaping leaders through adversity. Just as David trusted in the Lord and found strength in his struggles, so too must we embrace our journey with faith, courage, and perseverance.

In my journey, trusting God as my guide has meant relying on His strength to face my fears, grow through setbacks, and have faith in the path He is unfolding before me. Our stories share a divine truth: transformation is not only about reclaiming lost hope but about stepping boldly into the strength God has placed within us. "But those who hope in the Lord will renew their strength. They will soar on wings like eagles; they will run and not grow weary, they will walk and not be faint." (Isaiah 40:31, NIV)

A Call to Action

By aligning my personal journey with the powerful message of '*Go Take It Back!*' and the transformational story of David, I am reminded that every challenge is an opportunity for renewal. Just as David rose from despair to victory, we too are called to rise, reclaim, and walk boldly in our God-given purpose. "For I know the plans I have for you," declares the Lord, "plans to prosper you and not to harm you, plans to give you hope and a future." (Jeremiah 29:11, KJV)

Hope is not meant to be passively awaited but courageously pursued. Biblical hope is the confident expectation and assurance that God will do what He has promised. "Reclaim hope" means to take back or restore a sense of expectation that has been lost, often after facing hardship, trauma, or disillusionment. It reflects a conscious choice to believe again in the possibility of a better future, even after experiencing pain or setbacks. The phrase carries a sense of empowerment and healing, whether used in a personal, emotional, or broader social context. It suggests that hope, though once lost, stolen or diminished, can be rediscovered and embraced once more.

This is your moment to rewrite your story, to turn every setback into a setup for something greater. *Go take it back.* Your story, like mine and David's is a testimony of faith, resilience, and the unstoppable power of God's promises. "Do not fear, for I am with you; do not be dismayed, for I am your God. I will strengthen you and help you; I will uphold you with my righteous right hand." (Isaiah 41:10, NIV)

Step forward in faith. The victory is already yours!

Chapter 1 :
Contextual Analysis of David's Life

—————— 99 ——————

David's journey, from a humble shepherd boy to a celebrated king, is a narrative rich with layers of transformation, spiritual growth, and human complexity. His life, a tapestry interwoven with moments of rejection (1 Samuel 16:11), divine intervention (1 Samuel 16:13), triumph (1 Samuel 17:50), and setbacks (2 Samuel 12:10-14), offers profound insights into personal development and leadership.

This chapter unpacks some key stages of David's journey, delves into their deeper meanings, and highlights how these experiences can inform and inspire our own lives, reclaiming hope and victory over despair and defeat (Psalm 23:4; Psalm 51:10-12).

Rejection and Obscurity

David's formative years were characterised by obscurity and a lack of recognition, as even his own family failed to acknowledge his potential (1 Samuel 16:11). His humble occupation as a shepherd, seemingly insignificant by worldly standards, concealed the divine preparation at work in his life. Yet, these years of solitude were not in vain; rather, they served as a crucible in which he cultivated an intimate devotion to God (Psalm 23:1-4), unwavering courage (1 Samuel 17:34-37), and steadfast dependence on divine providence. This period underscores a recurring biblical principle: seasons of obscurity and rejection often serve as providential training grounds for future calling and leadership (James 1:2-4; Luke 16:10).

Real Life Applications

Embracing the Hidden Seasons

In the course of life, there are times when your abilities and contributions go unnoticed, leaving you feeling overlooked or unappreciated. Yet, these hidden seasons are not without purpose. Just as David spent years tending sheep before he was anointed as king (1 Samuel 16:11-13), such periods serve as vital opportunities for personal growth before being appointed. They cultivate inner strength, resilience, and the character needed for greater responsibilities that lie ahead. Rather than viewing these moments as stagnation, they can be embraced as essential preparation for what is to come.

Building Character Away from the Spotlight: The virtues cultivated in times of obscurity: patience, humility, and perseverance are foundational for long-term success. Scripture underscores this principle, as seen in Joseph's journey from imprisonment to leadership (Genesis 39:20-41:41) and in Jesus' formative years before His public ministry (Luke 2:52).

These hidden seasons refine character and equip us for the greater purpose ahead. Hebrews 12:11 (KJV) reminds that, "Now no chastening for the present seemeth to be joyous, but grievous: nevertheless, afterward it yieldeth the peaceable fruit of righteousness unto them which are exercised thereby."

A Divine Calling

The turning point in David's life came with his anointing by the prophet Samuel. This act was not just a ritual but a declaration of a divine calling that set him apart from the ordinary. The anointing underscored that his life had a purpose beyond what human judgment could dictate. However, this calling was not a guarantee of immediate triumph; it was a promise of a destiny that required faith, perseverance, character refining and continual growth.

Recognising Your Own Calling: You may experience an intrinsic sense of purpose, even in the absence of external affirmation. This inner calling, often understood as divine prompting, serves as a guiding force through periods of uncertainty. The Apostle Paul emphasises that God equips each person with unique gifts and a specific purpose (Romans 12:6; Ephesians 2:10). Moreover, the prophet Jeremiah was assured of his calling before birth, highlighting the divine intentionality behind personal vocations (Jeremiah 1:5).

Patience in the Process: The fulfilment of purpose is not immediate but unfolds through a process that requires perseverance. The biblical narrative of David exemplifies this principle. Though anointed as king in his youth (1 Samuel 16:12-13), David endured years of trials and preparation before assuming the throne. Similarly, we are called to exhibit steadfast patience, as articulated in James 1:2-4, which underscores the role of endurance in spiritual maturity.

Public Triumph Followed by Jealousy

David's victory over Goliath is emblematic of sudden public triumph, a moment when a once overlooked individual becomes a national hero. Yet, with this newfound fame came unforeseen challenges. King Saul's jealousy transformed what should have been a time of celebration into a period of intense persecution and exile. This juxtaposition reveals a crucial truth: public success often invites both admiration and envy, and true leadership is tested not only in victory but also in the face of adversity.

Handling Success with Grace and Navigating Criticism: A Biblical Perspective

Success and recognition should be approached with humility and a steadfast focus on long-term purpose rather than being influenced by the shifting opinions of others. Proverbs 27:2 (KJV) advises, "Let another praise you, and not your own mouth; a stranger, and not your own lips," highlighting the virtue of humility in moments of achievement. Furthermore, Philippians 2:3 (NIV) encourages believers to act with humility, stating, "Do nothing out of selfish ambition or vain conceit. Rather, in humility value others above yourselves."

Similarly, facing criticism and envy requires spiritual discernment and reliance on faith rather than external validation. The life of David offers a profound lesson in resilience, as seen in 1 Samuel 30:6 (NIV), where despite great distress, "David strengthened himself in the Lord his God." His example demonstrates the importance of seeking divine guidance rather than being swayed by negativity. Jesus Himself reinforces this principle in Matthew 5:11-12, reminding His followers that enduring opposition for righteousness' sake leads to eternal reward.

By maintaining humility in success and steadfastness in adversity, we align with biblical wisdom, ensuring that both triumphs and trials serve as opportunities for spiritual growth and fulfilment of purpose.

Strategic Alliances with the Enemy

David came to be in Philistine while fleeing from King Saul, who sought to kill him out of jealousy. After years of evading Saul's pursuit, David sought refuge with Achish, the king of Gath, a major Philistine city. To gain favour, David pretended to be loyal to the Philistines and even feigned madness at one point. Eventually, Achish granted him the town of Ziklag, where David and his men lived while conducting raids against enemy tribes. Though the Philistines trusted him, they ultimately refused to let him fight alongside them against Israel, fearing he might betray them in battle.

David's decision to seek refuge among the Philistines (1 Samuel 27) demonstrates the delicate and complicated balance between survival and faith. Despite aligning himself temporarily with Israel's enemies, he remained loyal to God's purpose and did not compromise his values.

Other Biblical Examples

Joseph in Egypt (Genesis 39-50)

Joseph, sold into slavery in Egypt, adapted to a foreign culture while remaining faithful to God. He served Pharaoh but used his position to save his family and many others from famine. His story teaches us that even in unfamiliar or hostile environments, we can remain faithful to God's plan.

Esther in Persia (Esther 4-8)

Esther, a Jewish woman, became queen of Persia, a nation that could have been hostile to her people. She navigated the palace politics carefully and used her influence to save the Jewish people from destruction. Her story highlights wisdom, courage, and faith in difficult circumstances.

Daniel in Babylon (Daniel 1-6)

Daniel and his friends were taken to Babylon and placed in the king's service. Though they worked within a pagan system, they remained unwavering in their devotion to God, refusing to compromise their faith. Their wisdom and integrity allowed them to have great influence while staying faithful to God.

How We Can Apply This Today

Wisdom in Decision-Making – Just as David encountered complex situations requiring careful choices, we too may face moments where the right path is unclear. In such times, seeking God's guidance through prayer and the counsel of wise mentors can help us make decisions that align with His will.

Integrity in Difficult Situations – Whether in our workplaces, schools, or personal relationships, we may find ourselves interacting with individuals who do not share our beliefs. Like Daniel, we can remain steadfast in our values while engaging with others in a way that is respectful and honourable.

Faith Over Fear – There may be moments, like those faced by Esther, when speaking up or making a difficult choice carries significant risk. Trusting in God's sovereignty empowers us to act with courage, knowing that He is in control.

Just as David relied on wisdom and trust in God to navigate his challenges, we too can approach life's difficulties with discernment, integrity, and unwavering faith.

Additional Real-Life Applications

Pragmatism in Difficult Situations: Life often forces us to make choices that are less than ideal. Just as David, when pursued by Saul, navigated difficult choices with discernment (1 Samuel 21-24), we too must consider all angles and adapt while remaining faithful to God's guidance. "The prudent see danger and take refuge, but the simple keep going and pay the penalty" (Proverbs 27:12, NIV).

Integrity Under Pressure: Even when circumstances demand compromises, maintaining personal integrity is essential. David's example reminds us that even in uncertain situations, our decisions can be guided by steadfast principles. Psalm 15:2 states that someone who lives with integrity does what is right, speaks honestly and sincerely, doesn't gossip, harm others, or insult anyone. David exemplified this commitment to integrity by choosing righteousness over convenience, echoing the wisdom of Proverbs 21:3 (NIV): "To do what is right and just is more acceptable to the Lord than sacrifice."

However, David's attempt to join the Philistine army and his subsequent rejection is a significant moment in his journey. This event, recorded in 1 Samuel 29-30, highlights themes of divine intervention, leadership, and personal crisis.

As mentioned above, David, while fleeing from King Saul, sought refuge among the Philistines under Achish, king of Gath. Achish trusted David and even wanted him to join the Philistine army against Israel.

However, the Philistine commanders objected, fearing that David might turn against them in battle. Their concern was valid. David had a strong history with Israel, having slain Goliath, a Philistine champion, and being celebrated in Israelite songs, "Saul has slain his thousands, and David his ten thousand." (1 Samuel 18:7, KJV).

This rejection was providential because:

- It prevented David from fighting against his own people. Had he fought Israel, it could have damaged his future claim to Israel's throne.
- It preserved David's reputation among the Israelites, ensuring he would later be accepted as king.
- It redirected David's focus to a personal crisis, the destruction of Ziklag

Crushing Setback at Ziklag

After David and his 600 soldiers were rejected from joining the Philistine army and endured a long, exhausting journey home under the scorching sun, they arrived in Ziklag, not to a warm welcome or the comforts of home, but to complete devastation.

In the scorched aftermath of Ziklag's devastation, a sombre darkness settled over David's camp. The once proud town, an oasis of refuge and unity now lay in ruins, its ashes echoing the heartbreak of its people. Families were torn apart; wives and children had been seized by the relentless Amalekites. In the immediate despair, grief mingled with a burning anger that targeted the very man who was meant to be their protector.

David's men, their eyes reflecting both sorrow and fury, looked upon their leader with a mix of betrayal and desperation. Their homes, lives, and futures had been shattered. In a moment of collective anguish, murmurs of retribution began to swell into a clamour: some even urged that David be held accountable and stoned for the calamity that had befallen them. It was as if the physical destruction of their city had found a human target upon which to exact their unbridled grief and despair.

The Weight of Leadership

This tumultuous episode was not merely about the loss of physical structures or kin; it was an existential test of leadership. David, a man whose past was marked by both triumphs and tribulations, now found himself confronting the raw edge of human emotion. In the face of such intense despair, the suggestion of stoning was not just an attack on his person.

It was an indictment of his authority and, in the eyes of his followers, his failure to protect them. Yet in this crucible of despair, David's response would be decisive. His measured silence, his refusal to be swept up by the mob's vengeance, underscored a deeper commitment to justice rather than mere retribution.

In that fraught moment, the very essence of leadership was on trial: could one, burdened with the weight of loss, rise above the instinct for immediate vengeance and instead chart a course toward redemption? David's inner resolve, forged through years of hardship and divine guidance, began to manifest as he prepared to act, not as a tyrant who shirked blame, but as a leader who would restore hope.

His decision to pursue the Amalekites, to reclaim what had been lost, was not just a military manoeuvre; it was a statement that true leadership requires taking responsibility, bearing the cost of collective sorrow and transforming it into a path for renewal. It was one of the most harrowing moments in David's journey, the devastation he encountered at Ziklag.

This crisis, though painful, became a pivotal turning point. It forced David to confront loss and despair, and in doing so, deepened his reliance on divine guidance. Rather than succumbing to defeat, he used this setback as a catalyst for recovery and future triumph, illustrating that even our lowest moments can be springboards for growth.

David showed strong leadership by:

- **Turning to God for guidance** – He sought divine direction through the **ephod** and was told to pursue the Amalekites.

- **Encouraging his men** – Despite their grief, he rallied them for battle.

- **Recovering all that was lost** – They defeated the Amalekites and rescued their families.

Real Life Applications

Setbacks, both personal and professional, are unavoidable in life. Yet, within these moments of hardship lies the potential for transformation. For example, David's time at Ziklag serves as a powerful reminder that failure does not have to be the end of the road. Rather, it can be a turning point, a chance to reassess, rebuild, and emerge stronger than before. What may seem like defeat can instead become the foundation for renewal and growth.

Resilience is often forged in the fires of adversity. When faced with overwhelming challenges, the ability to seek inner strength can make all the difference. Whether through unwavering faith, the support of a trusted community, or deep self-reflection, the path forward is often illuminated by the courage to look beyond despair. It is in these moments of crisis that individuals discover their true capacity to rise again, transforming setbacks into stepping stones toward a greater future.

Preparation for Divine Purpose

The overarching theme of David's life is one of deliberate preparation. Every phase, be it obscurity, divine calling, public triumph, exile, and setback, was integral to shaping him into the leader he was destined to become. David's experiences underscore a fundamental truth: greatness is not the result of a single moment of glory but the cumulative outcome of enduring trials, persistent faith, and the continuous honing of character.

Long-Term Vision Over Immediate Results: The life of David exemplifies how small, faithful steps lead to fulfilling one's God-given destiny. Here are some scriptural references that reinforce this idea:

David's Preparation in the Fields – "He chose David his servant and took him from the sheepfolds; from following the ewes that had young, He brought him to shepherd Jacob His people, and Israel His inheritance." (Psalm 78:70-71, NKJV). David's journey began with humble beginnings as a shepherd, where he developed skills that later helped him as king.

Faithfulness in Small Things – "Whoever can be trusted with very little can also be trusted with much, and whoever is dishonest with very little will also be dishonest with much." (Luke 16:10, NIV). Success often starts with small, faithful steps, just as David's obedience in the small tasks led to greater responsibilities.

Facing Challenges with Courage – "David said, 'The Lord who rescued me from the paw of the lion and the paw of the bear will rescue me from the hand of this Philistine.'" (1 Samuel 17:37, NIV). David's past experiences prepared him to face Goliath, showing that small victories build up to great triumphs. "The path of the righteous is like the morning sun, shining ever brighter till the full light of day." (Proverbs 4:18, NIV). Our journeys unfold gradually, just as David's anointing as king took years to be fully realised.

Endurance and Waiting on God's Timing – "Wait for the Lord; be strong and take heart and wait for the Lord." (Psalm 27:14, NIV). David had to wait many years after being anointed before he actually was appointed and became king, teaching us that perseverance is key to success. David's life teaches us that our destinies are not achieved in an instant but through consistent faith, **effort, and trust in God's timing.**

Embracing the Process of Growth

Whether in career, personal relationships, or spiritual life, every challenge we face can be a stepping stone toward a larger purpose if we are willing to learn and grow from it. As Romans 5:3-4 (NIV) reminds us, "Not only so, but we also glory in our sufferings, because we know that suffering produces perseverance; perseverance, character; and character, hope."

Each trial refines us, shaping us into who we are meant to be, just as James 1:2-4 encourages us to "consider it pure joy...whenever you face trials of many kinds, because you know that the testing of your faith produces perseverance." When we embrace the process of growth with faith, we align ourselves with God's greater plan for our lives.

Key Themes & Lessons

1. **Divine Intervention** – God orchestrated events so that David avoided an alliance that could have been disastrous.

2. **Leadership in Crisis** – David's response at Ziklag demonstrated resilience, faith, and wisdom.

3. **God's Faithfulness** – Even in hardship, David remained faithful and was ultimately restored.

This turning point ultimately strengthened David's position, leading him closer to becoming king of Israel after Saul's death.

David's life serves as a multifaceted blueprint for understanding how divine purpose and human experience intertwine. From the unnoticed moments of obscurity to the trials of exile and the complexities of moral decisions, his journey offers a rich tapestry of lessons. These lessons remind us that every phase, no matter how challenging or insignificant it may seem, is part of a larger narrative of growth and purpose.

In our own lives, the story of David reminds us that rejection can be God's way of preparing us for something greater (1 Samuel 16:7). His journey teaches us that success is both a blessing and a test of character (2 Samuel 5:12), while setbacks can serve as opportunities for growth and divine refinement (Psalm 66:10). By trusting in God's plan and embracing every season; both trials and triumphs, we align ourselves with His purpose, ultimately achieving lasting and meaningful success according to His will (Jeremiah 29:11).

Chapter 2 :
Theological Insights and Applications

———————— 🙶 ————————

Divine Appointments Amidst Human Disappointments (Man's disappointments can be God's appointment)

Life's journey sometimes includes moments of rejection and disappointment. In 1 Samuel 29, David, who had taken refuge among the Philistines, encountered an unexpected rejection when their king, heeding counsel, denied him the chance to join the battle. While this may have appeared to be yet another setback in David's challenging path, it was, in truth, divine redirection.

God often orchestrates events that seem unfavourable to us, not as punishment, but as protection. "For my thoughts are not your thoughts, neither are your ways my ways, declares the Lord" (Isaiah 55:8, NIV). If David had gone to battle with the Philistines, he might have been forced into an impossible moral conflict, fighting against his own people, Israel. Instead, God used this rejection to position David for a greater purpose: the rescue of his own people from the Amalekite invasion (1 Samuel 29–30). "And we know that in all things God works for the good of those who love him, who have been called according to his purpose" (Romans 8:28, NIV).

This principle holds true in our lives today. Sometimes, what appears to be rejection is actually God's hand shielding us from compromise or greater harm. When doors close unexpectedly, it is often because God is guiding us to something better. Proverbs 3:5-6 reminds us to trust in the Lord with all our hearts and lean not on our own understanding, for He directs our paths.

The Enemy Strikes at Moments of Vulnerability

As David and his men were navigating their dismissal from the Philistine camp, another crisis was unfolding, as pointed out in the previous chapter. The Amalekites seized the opportunity to attack Ziklag, their home, burning it to the ground and taking their families captive (1 Samuel 30:1-2). This highlights a crucial spiritual reality: the enemy often strikes when we are distracted, weary, or vulnerable.

Jesus warned of this tactic in Matthew 13:25 (KJV) , where He spoke of how, "While men slept, the enemy came and sowed tares among the wheat." This is a reminder that spiritual vigilance is essential. The enemy does not wait for us to be strong; rather, he exploits moments when our guard is down. This principle applies not only to individual lives but also to families, churches, and communities. This parable further illustrates how spiritual enemies work under the cover of distraction, apathy, or ignorance, infiltrating and corrupting what is meant for good.

"The devil, your adversary, prowls like a roaring lion, seeking whom he may devour." (1 Peter 5:8, ESV). This verse is a powerful warning that spiritual opposition is real and active. The imagery of a roaring lion emphasises the enemy's cunning and relentless pursuit to weaken faith and lead believers astray. Therefore, stay vigilant in prayer and rooted in God's truth, resisting temptation with firm faith. What steps can you take today to strengthen your spiritual defences?

To counteract this strategy of the enemy, we must cultivate a lifestyle of prayer and spiritual awareness. Ephesians 6:10-11 exhorts us to be strong in the Lord and put on the full armour of God so that we can stand against the schemes of the devil. Even in times of weariness, maintaining spiritual disciplines such as prayer, fasting, and studying God's Word fortifies us against unexpected attacks.

The principle that the enemy strikes at moments of vulnerability is a recurring theme throughout Scripture. In 1 Samuel 30:1-6, the Amalekites attacked Ziklag while David and his men were away, taking advantage of their absence. This strategy highlights a fundamental tactic of both physical and spiritual warfare, attacking when defences are down.

Satan, referred to as the adversary (1 Peter 5:8), seeks opportune moments to strike, such as when Jesus was physically weak after fasting for 40 days (Matthew 4:1-11). Likewise, Judas betrayed Jesus at night, a time associated with secrecy and vulnerability (John 13:30).

Further Application

Guard Against Spiritual Weakness – Just as David's city was unprotected in his absence, we must remain spiritually alert. Times of exhaustion, discouragement, or complacency can invite attacks in the form of temptation, doubt, or deception. Regular prayer, Scripture study, and fellowship strengthen our defences.

Beware of Distraction – The enemy often exploits distraction to introduce sin or confusion. The parable of the sower (Matthew 13:18-23) shows how worries, riches, and pleasures can choke spiritual growth. Keeping focused on God's truth protects against subtle deception.

Stay Spiritually Awake – Jesus warned His disciples in Gethsemane, "Watch and pray, that ye enter not into temptation" (Matthew 26:41, KJV). Spiritual vigilance prevents being caught off guard by trials, temptations, or attacks.

Recover What Was Lost – When David discovered the attack on Ziklag, he sought God's direction and pursued the enemy (1 Samuel 30:7-8). Likewise, when the enemy attempts to steal joy, peace, or faith, we must actively reclaim these through prayer, repentance, faith and decisive action.

Support One Another – David's men were devastated by the attack, but he strengthened himself in the Lord (1 Samuel 30:6). Community support and encouragement in faith are vital during moments of spiritual warfare. However, there are times when we must find resilience in solitude, relying solely on God's strength. Even Jesus, in His most trying moments, prayed alone while His disciples slept (Matthew 26:40-41), demonstrating that divine strength sustains us when human support fails.

The enemy always looks for unguarded moments to strike, whether through sin, discouragement, or external circumstances. Recognising this tactic allows us to remain vigilant, rooted in faith, and proactive in spiritual defence. Through prayer, discernment, and reliance on God, we can resist attacks and emerge victorious!

Managing Healthy Grieving

When David and his men returned to Ziklag and saw the destruction and loss, they were overwhelmed with grief. Intense grief is a profound and overwhelming emotional response to significant loss, often encompassing deep sorrow, anguish, and despair. This form of grief can manifest physically, emotionally, and mentally, affecting an individual's overall well-being.

The grief experienced by David's men is worth exploring in more depth here. Men may experience grief often influenced by societal expectations and traditional gender stereotypes and perceptions of masculinity. Research indicates that men are less likely to express their emotions or seek support during bereavement. They may exhibit anger, engage in risk-taking behaviours, or immerse themselves in work or practical tasks as coping mechanisms. Some men might also turn to substances like alcohol or drugs to manage or numb their feelings. These unhealthy patterns can lead to physical health issues and destructive behaviours.

Mental Health Concerns

In 2023, England and Wales experienced a stark and troubling rise in suicide rates, registering the highest number of suicides since 1999. A total of 6,069 suicides were formally recorded, reflecting a rate of 11.4 deaths per 100,000 people. This figure marks an increase from the 5,642 suicides reported in 2022 and underscores a growing public health concern surrounding mental health and suicide prevention in the UK (Office for National Statistics, 2024).

This upward trend is disproportionately affecting men. Of the total suicides in 2023, approximately three-quarters were male, with 4,506 male deaths compared to 1,563 among females. This gender disparity in suicide mortality has been a persistent feature of UK suicide statistics, reinforcing the urgent need for gender-sensitive mental health interventions and support systems (Office for National Statistics, 2024).

The data further reveals that the highest age-specific suicide rate was observed among males aged 45 to 49, reaching 25.5 deaths per 100,000 population. This demographic has consistently demonstrated elevated risk, often attributed to a complex interplay of socio-economic pressures, mental health challenges, and limited help-seeking behaviour among middle-aged men (Office for National Statistics, 2024).

Media outlets have also highlighted this alarming trend. *The Guardian*, in its coverage of the official statistics, echoed the concern, emphasizing the rise to 6,069 deaths as a critical public health issue and noting that this figure represents the highest rate recorded since the end of the 20th century (*The Guardian*, 2024).

Depression, a major contributor to these rising suicide rates, remains an often underdiagnosed condition in men. Many men are reluctant to seek help for mental health issues, which can lead to symptoms being overlooked or misunderstood. Rather than expressing sadness or despair, men may exhibit irritability, aggression, and risk-taking behaviours, which are less commonly associated with depression. This contributes to the difficulty in identifying and treating the condition.

Emerging evidence highlights the critical need to address mental health challenges among men, particularly in later adulthood. Statistics indicate that approximately one in five men will experience major depression by the age of 65; however, many endure these struggles in silence, either unaware of the mental health services available to them or hesitant to seek assistance due to prevailing societal stigmas (Counselling Directory, 2024). This reluctance to engage with mental health support is compounded by rising suicide rates, which further emphasise the urgency of comprehensive public health interventions. According to the Office for National Statistics (2023), men accounted for around three-quarters of all suicides in England and Wales in 2022, a figure that has remained relatively consistent over the past decade. These data underscore the imperative for greater awareness, early identification, and culturally sensitive support strategies aimed at improving mental health outcomes among men.

Suicide remains a significant public health concern in the UK, with men under 50 being the most affected group. It is the leading cause of death for men in this age range, with factors such as societal pressures, financial instability, and reluctance to discuss mental health contributing to this alarming statistic. According to the Samaritans, traditional expectations around masculinity often discourage men from seeking help, leading to increased isolation and distress.

Research indicates that men from lower socio-economic backgrounds are disproportionately affected by suicide, with increased vulnerability stemming from factors such as financial hardship, unemployment, and social marginalisation. According to the Samaritans (2023), the relationship between socio-economic disadvantage and suicide risk is clear, with those experiencing poverty facing some of the highest rates of suicide. The charity emphasises that suicide is not inevitable and that prevention is achievable through coordinated efforts to address risk factors, improve mental health support, and strengthen protective measures. Critical strategies include early intervention, the expansion of accessible and culturally sensitive support services, and concerted efforts to challenge and change societal attitudes toward mental health, particularly within male populations who may be less likely to seek help due to stigma and traditional gender norms.

The Bible also includes practical examples of how you can grieve. Efforts to address this crisis can be found within the biblical message of hope and support for those in distress. The Bible encourages individuals to seek help and lean on community support, as seen in verses like Galatians 6:2 (NIV, which states, "Carry each other's burdens, and in this way you will fulfil the law of Christ." This emphasises the importance of supporting one another in times of hardship, highlighting that no one needs to face life's challenges alone. With a focus on faith, support, and community, these principles can help provide comfort and guidance to those struggling with suicidal thoughts.

The Bible acknowledges the depth of human sorrow. Here in 1 Samuel 30:4 (ESV), it is recorded that David and his men "wept until they had no more strength to weep," illustrating that expressing profound grief is a natural and human response, not a sign of weakness. As their grief evolved from loud weeping to silence, it did not signify closure but rather the depth of sorrow, so profound that it defied words or verbal expression.

Recognising and addressing intense grief in men especially, is crucial given the above statistics. Encouraging open conversations about emotions, challenging traditional notions of toxic masculinity, and providing accessible spiritual and mental health support can help mitigate the adverse effects of grief and reduce the risk of depression and suicide among men.

The Process of Grief in Leadership

Leadership does not exempt one from grief, nor does faith make us immune to sorrow. Throughout the Bible, we see great men and women of God experiencing profound grief. In the Garden of Gethsemane, Jesus Himself faced overwhelming sorrow, saying, "My soul is exceedingly sorrowful, even to death" (Mark 14:34, NKJV). His agony was so intense that He sweat drops of blood (Luke 22:44), demonstrating the depth of His suffering as He prepared to bear the weight of the world's sin.

Elijah, after his great victory on Mount Carmel, fell into deep despair and wished for death (1 Kings 19:4). Paul spoke of the crushing hardships he endured, saying he was burdened beyond measure, even despairing of life itself (2 Corinthians 1:8). Even

Jesus, the Son of God, wept at the tomb of Lazarus (John 11:35), showing His deep compassion and sorrow.

Grief and sorrow are not signs of weakness but are often part of the journey of faith. Just as Jesus found strength through prayer and submission to the Father's will, we, too, can bring our burdens before God, knowing that He understands our pain and sustains us through every trial.

However, grief is not meant to be a permanent state, instead it is a process. David exemplified resilience; after mourning, he turned to God for strength and direction. As mentioned earlier, 1 Samuel 30:6 (NKJV) tells us that "David strengthened himself in the Lord his God." This is a key lesson for us: while grief is natural, it should ultimately lead us back to God, who is our refuge and strength (Psalm 46:1).

Moving forward from grief or closure does not mean ignoring pain but rather allowing God to heal and restore. David's story did not end in despair; through divine guidance, he pursued the Amalekites and recovered everything that was taken. This demonstrates that even in our lowest moments, God is able to restore what has been lost (Joel 2:25), giving hope after despair.

The story of David's rejection, vulnerability, and grief teaches us profound theological lessons that are applicable to our lives today. Rejection is often divine redirection, the enemy seeks to strike at moments of weakness, and while grieving is necessary, it is not permanent. Grief is a natural response to loss, often described through Kübler-Ross's (1969) five-stage model: denial, anger, bargaining, depression, and acceptance. These stages represent common emotional reactions but do not necessarily occur in a fixed order or apply universally. While influential, the model has faced criticism for oversimplifying the complexity and individuality of the grieving process.

While we may journey through the various stages of grief, there inevitably comes a time when the process of closure must begin; recognizing that closure is not a fixed endpoint or destination, but rather an ongoing process and personal progression. Throughout every trial and season of loss, the sovereignty of God remains constant, offering guidance, hope, and the promise of restoration. As we face our own disappointments and struggles, may we, like David, find strength in the Lord and trust in His faithful purpose for our lives.

Leadership, Grief, and Resilience

In 1 Samuel 30:4, we read that "David and his men wept aloud until they had no strength left to weep." This moment occurred when David and his men returned to Ziklag, only to find their city burned and their families taken captive. Despite being warriors and leaders, they experienced deep grief, demonstrating that leadership does not shield one from sorrow. However, what sets great leaders apart is their ability to process grief and find the resilience to move forward.

Leadership often requires individuals to make difficult decisions, endure setbacks, and face losses. Many biblical leaders exemplified this reality as mentioned earlier:

- **Elijah**: After his dramatic confrontation with the prophets of Baal, Elijah fled in fear and despair, even asking God to take his life (1 Kings 19:4). Yet, after rest and divine reassurance, he continued his prophetic mission.

- **Paul**: Faced with imprisonment, beatings, and rejection, Paul expressed sorrow in his letters (2 Corinthians 1:8), but his faith and purpose drove him forward.

- **Jesus**: In moments like weeping over Lazarus (John 11:35) and His agony in Gethsemane (Luke 22:44), Jesus openly expressed grief. Nevertheless, He remained committed to His mission, demonstrating that sorrow and perseverance coexist.

The Cultural Stigma Around Men Expressing Emotion

In many societies, men are conditioned to suppress emotions, particularly sadness. Expressions including "real men don't cry", "man up" or "Take it like a man!" are deeply ingrained in various cultures, reinforcing the stereotype that emotional expression is a sign of weakness. This aligns with broader discussions of toxic masculinity, which discourages vulnerability in men, often leading to emotional repression, anger, mental health struggles, and unhealthy coping mechanisms for example addictions or becoming workaholics. This is so important that it is worth repeating.

However, biblical narratives challenge the notion of toxic masculinity. If great leaders like David, Elijah, Paul, and Jesus openly displayed sorrow, then it is clear that strength is not in suppression but in resilience; the ability to grieve, process, and move forward.

Resilience: The Key to Moving Forward

Resilience is not the absence of emotion but the ability to recover from hardship. David, after weeping, sought God's guidance (1 Samuel 30:6-8), took action, and recovered what was lost. His example teaches us that true leadership acknowledges pain but does not remain paralyzed by it.

The biblical examples of David and others show that grief is a universal human experience, not a weakness. In leadership, the key is not avoidance of sorrow but the strength to rise after it. A cultural shift is therefore needed to revisit masculinity, allowing space for men to express emotion without fear of judgment; minimising, over-spiritualising or trivialising their pain if, as and when they reach out for help. By embracing resilience, regardless of the capacity in which we serve or our sphere of influence, we can navigate grief in a healthy and constructive way.

The Fellowship of Suffering

David and his men returned to Ziklag only to find it burned and their families taken captive by the Amalekites. This was a moment of intense suffering for all. The men "wept until they had no more strength to weep" (1 Samuel 30:4, NLT), yet in their anguish, they turned against David and spoke of stoning him (1 Samuel 30:6). Their pain blinded them to the fact that David, too, was grieving the loss of his own family and possessions.

This passage highlights a profound truth: suffering can either divide people or bring them together. Unfortunately, instead of uniting with David in grief, the men turned on him. They expressed their grief in anger. That was part of their grieving process.

The five stages or non-linear process of grief: denial, anger, bargaining, depression, and acceptance, represent the emotional journey from shock and resistance to eventual understanding and coming to terms with loss.

However, David responded differently. He strengthened himself in the Lord (1 Samuel 30:6) and sought God's guidance rather than retaliating against his men. His trust in God not only restored his faith but also led to the recovery of all that was lost (1 Samuel 30:18-19).

The Fickleness of David's Men at Ziklag

In this chapter, the narrative thrust centres on a tragic event at Ziklag, where an Amalekite raid results in the devastating loss of wives, children, and the burning of their city. Amid this calamity, David stands not only as a leader but also as a man deeply wounded by the same tragedy that has befallen his people. However, rather than uniting in mutual grief and support, his men direct their anguish outward, blaming David for the catastrophe, questioning his decisions, and failing to recognise that the calamity was beyond his control. Their fickleness is striking; when personal and communal loss strike hard, loyalties shift, and emotions turn toward scapegoating.

The Fickleness of Loyalty and the Burden of Blame

David's men, overwhelmed by the shock and despair of losing their families and community, quickly seek someone to hold accountable. Their reaction is not so much an informed critique of leadership but rather a desperate need to find a cause for their suffering. In moments of crisis, it is not uncommon for us to channel grief and fear into anger, often targeting the visible symbol of leadership, in this case, David. Their rapid shift from loyalty to blame exemplifies the human tendency to recoil from leaders during hardships, forgetting that these leaders, too, are susceptible to pain and loss.

This event foreshadows the principle found in the New Testament: we are called to share in one another's sufferings rather than isolate or attack each other.

Bearing One Another's Burdens: Paul exhorts believers to "Bear ye one another's burdens, and so fulfil the law of Christ" (Galatians 6:2. KJV). Instead of distancing ourselves from those who are suffering, we are called to actively support and uplift them. By shouldering their burdens, we reflect Christ's love and care, offering not only emotional and spiritual support but also practical help. This selfless, empathetic act of bearing one another's burdens fosters unity and creates a community where love and grace can thrive, fulfilling the heart of Christ's law. Yet each one is admonished to carry his own load.

Weeping with Those Who Weep: "Rejoice with those who rejoice, weep with those who weep." (Romans 12:15, ESV). David's men failed to recognise that he was also suffering. Their grief became self-focused, leading them to anger rather than solidarity. True fellowship means recognising the shared weight of sorrow.

Encouraging and Strengthening One Another: In 1 Thessalonians 5:11 (ESV), Paul writes: "Therefore encourage one another and build one another up, just as you are doing." Rather than breaking each other down in times of distress, we must provide strength and encouragement, just as David later did for his men.

The Example of Christ in Suffering: Jesus Himself is the ultimate example of sharing in suffering. "Surely He has borne our griefs and carried our sorrows." (Isaiah 53:4, NKJV). Just as Christ bore our pain, we, too, should be willing to bear the burdens of others in love and compassion.

How we can share in the suffering of others? Let us look at these in a bit more detail.

In the midst of pain and hardship, it is crucial to approach others with empathy rather than judgment. When David's men were suffering, they unfairly judged him, but instead of turning blame toward leadership or others, we must seek to understand the struggles that individuals are facing. Rather than making assumptions, we are called to embrace a posture of compassion and openness.

In moments of suffering, one of the most profound responses is to turn to prayer and encouragement. David exemplified this by seeking God and finding strength in Him during his own trials. Likewise, when someone we know is grieving, we should not only pray for them but also pray with them, offering spiritual and emotional support that bolsters their strength in the face of adversity.

Furthermore, rather than dividing us, suffering should draw us closer together. By recognising that every individual carries his or her own burdens, we foster an environment of compassion and empathy. In this shared experience of human vulnerability, we can create unity, setting aside resentment or division, and instead embracing solidarity in our collective struggles.

Finally, practical support plays an indispensable role in walking alongside those in grief. Whether through offering physical help, providing financial assistance, or simply being present, we must actively engage in acts of kindness that demonstrate our care and commitment. These tangible expressions of support are often as healing as any words we can offer, creating a foundation of comfort amidst sorrow.

The story of David at Ziklag teaches us that suffering is a shared experience, and in those moments, we must support one another rather than turn to blame, criticism and judgement. The biblical principle of bearing one another's burdens (Galatians 6:2) reminds us that true fellowship is found in walking together through trials with empathy, encouragement, and love. Just as Christ shared in our suffering, we are called to do the same for one another.

Chapter 3 :
Seeking Divine Direction at Ziklag

—————— 99 ——————

Amid hardships and turmoil, a moment of profound crisis unfolded the day the cherished town of Ziklag fell to a sudden and ruthless assault. The Amalekites, fierce and merciless, swept through the unsuspecting settlement, leaving destruction, anguish, and an urgent call to action in their wake. In the depths of this despair, David rose not just as a warrior but as a leader whose heart was steadfastly aligned with divine direction.

The Tragedy at Ziklag

Ziklag was more than a strategic outpost; it was a home and haven for David's people, a place where hope and community intertwined. When the Amalekites struck, they did not only seize goods or burn structures; they captured the families, the wives, and the children, scattering a people's future into the winds of captivity. The land, once filled with the murmurs of daily life, now echoed with the anguished cries of those left behind. For David, the loss was not merely tactical; it was a wound to the soul of his leadership, a call to act in the midst of overwhelming sorrow.

Redemption Amid the Ashes

This episode at Ziklag extends beyond its immediate historical and cultural context, offering profound insights into the nature of collective suffering and the essence of true leadership. Its narrative

(1 Samuel 30) encapsulates the tension between despair and resilience, as the people, overwhelmed by grief and loss, sought to cast blame upon David. Their impulse to stone him was not merely an act of anger but a desperate plea for stability, an attempt to externalise the weight of their affliction.

David's response, however, redefined leadership in moments of crisis. Rather than succumbing to fear or retaliation, he strengthened himself in the Lord (1 Samuel 30:6), demonstrating a model of governance that does not merely react to suffering but seeks transformation through it. In doing so, he redirected the trajectory of his people, illustrating that true leadership does not avoid hardship but navigates through it with faith and resolve.

Thus, while the flames of Ziklag consumed the physical city, they also served as a crucible for renewal. Out of betrayal and devastation, a leader emerged, one who transcended the anguish of the present to guide his people toward restoration and divine purpose. This episode stands as an enduring testament to the challenges of leadership in the face of overwhelming adversity, emphasising the redemptive potential found within suffering when met with faith and steadfastness.

A Leader in Deep Agony

In the quiet aftermath of the attack, as the smoke of ruin drifted over the wilderness, David's heart was heavy with mourning. His men, though brave, looked to him not only for military command but for a beacon of hope in a dark hour. In that moment of desolation, David's spirit wrestled with the enormity of the loss. Yet it was precisely this vulnerability that opened his heart to a singular truth: true leadership is rooted in humility and dependence on the Almighty.

David's mind recalled the countless times he had witnessed God's hand in the most unexpected moments. The memory of past deliverances, the miracles that had punctuated his life, fortified his resolve. Yet, with every step he took, he was acutely aware that human strength alone could not restore what had been lost. The task ahead demanded something greater, a divine strategy and a spiritual reckoning.

Turning to the Divine: The Act of Seeking Guidance

In the silence of that fateful moment, David turned to God whilst his men were in anguish and despair. With eyes turned upward and his heart steeped in earnest prayer, he sought the counsel of God. This was not a decision made from mere strategy, but one forged in the crucible of faith.

In my book, '*Safely Through on Broken Pieces- Focus on What You Have Left, Not on What You Have Lost*', I pointed out a similar experience. Paul's journey to Rome, as described in Acts 27, presents a stark contrast between faith and fear. While the sailors and passengers on the ship panicked in the face of a violent storm, Paul sought God and received divine revelation.

Instead of succumbing to fear, he trusted in God's promise that all lives would be spared. His faith gave him calm assurance, allowing him to encourage others, saying, "Take heart, for I have faith in God that it will be exactly as I have been told" (Acts 27:25, ESV). This highlights the power of seeking God in crisis. While others despair, those who trust in Him receive peace and direction. Though they are not immune to fear and doubt, they choose to trust Him anyway, demonstrating that faith is not the absence of fear, but the courage to move forward despite it.

David approached God with a humble petition: "Shall we pursue the raiders? Will the Lord grant us victory and the recovery of all that was lost?" (1 Samuel 30:8, NKJV). His words were not a cry of defiance, but a prayer of submission, an acknowledgement that the battle was not his alone to fight. As it is written, "...for the battle is the Lord's, and He will give you into our hands" (1 Samuel 17:47, NKJV).

Likewise, when King Jehoshaphat faced a vast army, he prayed to the Lord. The Spirit of the Lord spoke through Jahaziel, declaring, "Do not be afraid or discouraged because of this vast army. For the battle is not yours, but God's" (2 Chronicles 20:15, NIV). In both cases, victory came not by human strength but by divine intervention.

His pursuit of divine guidance defined David's character. Instead of rushing into battle fuelled by anger or desperation, he paused to seek God's will. "Seek ye first the kingdom of God and His righteousness" (Matthew 6:33, KJV). This moment exemplified true spiritual leadership, a steadfast trust in a power far greater than earthly strength.

Rather than reacting in haste or out of raw emotion, David turned to God for guidance. There is a wise saying: 'When emotion is high, judgement is low!' and the converse is also true! He called for the ephod and inquired of the Lord, asking as mentioned, "Shall I pursue? Will I overtake?" (1 Samuel 30:8, NIV).

His questions were about taking action and ensuring that his steps aligned with God's will. David understood that not every battle was his to fight. Even in the face of personal devastation, he chose to seek divine wisdom before making a move.

The Danger of Acting Out of Emotion

In moments of crisis, our natural human response is to react, sometimes in anger, sometimes in desperation. Acting out of frustration, however, can lead to rash decisions with long-term consequences. How often do we make choices in the heat of the moment, only to regret them later? Wisdom requires discernment and patience, ensuring that our actions align with God's will rather than our fleeting emotions.

Choosing Your Battles Wisely

Not every conflict requires our participation. Just because a battle presents itself does not necessarily mean it is ours to fight. David sought God's direction before pursuing the enemy. In doing so, he avoided unnecessary struggle and ensured his efforts were not in vain. Likewise, we must learn to choose our battles wisely. Some fights are distractions, meant to drain our energy and divert us from our true purpose. Seeking divine direction helps us distinguish between battles that require our engagement and those we must leave in God's hands.

David's story teaches us a crucial lesson: before taking action, seek God. Proverbs 3:6 (KJV) reminds us, "In all thy ways acknowledge him, and he shall direct thy paths." Before making a decision, ask for divine direction. When we wait on the Lord, we move with confidence, knowing that our steps are ordered, our battles are chosen wisely, and our victory is assured.

The Divine Response: A Beacon of Assurance

In that sacred moment of intercession, a profound silence followed David's inquiry: a silence that was pregnant with divine promise. Whether through a still, small voice, a surge of inner conviction, or a sign in the unfolding of nature, the answer became unmistakable: Pursue!

God's reassurance came not with the bluster of worldly command, but with the gentle yet powerful assurance that victory and restoration were within reach. "Pursue them," the divine message resounded in David's heart, "for you shall overtake them, and all that was taken will be restored." (1 Samuel 30:8, NKJV).

Go, Catch, rescue!

The answer came swiftly and decisively:

"Pursue, for you shall surely overtake and recover all."

This response was transformative. It turned mourning into mission, despair into determination, and uncertainty into a steadfast belief that the Almighty was at work. It wasn't just permission to act. It was a guarantee of victory and restoration! God assured David that this battle was his to win, and the outcome was already decided. The victory is yours, provided you seek Divine will and purpose and obediently follow given direction! We are more than conquerors!

This divine direction gave David the confidence to move forward with clarity and purpose, rather than being driven by frustration or pain. David's resolve was renewed. Likewise, the hearts of his men were set aflame with hope. Divine deliverance was not just about reclaiming lost property. It reaffirmed the covenant between God and His people: a bond built on trust, obedience, and alignment with His will.

Mobilising the Troops: The Pursuit of the Amalekites

On this basis only, David swiftly organised his forces. He divided his 600 men into strategic units, each tasked with pursuing the scattered raiders through the rugged terrain of the wilderness. The pursuit was not just a military manoeuvre but a spiritual expedition.

Every step David and his warriors took was infused with the knowledge that they were instruments of a higher purpose, carrying out the will of God. No longer was there any mention of stoning David! Instead, there was a desire to rally behind their leader purposefully and with a clear sense of vision to pursue and recover all that was lost. They bought into the vision and now owned it. This was now personal.

There was hope after despair.

As they advanced, the soldiers found their courage bolstered by the memory of the divine promise. Their leader's unwavering faith was contagious, inspiring even the weariest and disheartened to press onward. In the heat of the pursuit, every challenge encountered, extreme fatigue, grief and loss after that demanding march back to Ziglag in the blazing sun, was met with the conviction that God's guidance was both present and potent.

Faith, Obedience, and Divine Partnership

The episode at Ziklag stands as a timeless chapter in the accounts of faith, a narrative that continues to inspire leaders and believers alike. David's approach, characterised by humility in the face of overwhelming loss and an unwavering commitment to seek God's counsel, offers profound lessons for every generation. His story teaches that true strength is found not in acting impulsively on one's own understanding, but in pausing to consult the source of all wisdom.

God didn't just give permission. He promised triumph and restoration! Just as He assured David that the battle was already won, He assures you today that victory is yours. Step forward in faith, for the outcome is secure! "In all these things we are more than conquerors through Him who loved us" (Romans 8:37, NKJV). Keep pressing on, for God goes before you, and His promises never fail! (Deuteronomy 31:8).

Chapter 4:
Faith-Driven Leadership and Strategy

—————— 99 ——————

Divine Strength and Victory Over Adversity

The moment when David "strengthened himself in the Lord" (1 Samuel 30:6, NKJV) before pursuing his enemies is a profound demonstration of the interplay between faith and action. This account reveals that true strength comes not from human might alone but from reliance on God. It reminds us that before we engage in life's battles, we must first seek divine empowerment.

David's journey was not defined solely by his skill as a warrior but by his deep trust in God. Time and again, Scripture reinforces the principle that spiritual fortification precedes external victory. Just as David sought God in distress, we are encouraged to do the same: "Be strong in the Lord and in the power of His might" (Ephesians 6:10, NKJV).

When faced with loss and opposition, David did not succumb to despair. Instead, he turned to God, finding strength to reclaim what was taken. His pursuit of the Amalekites, Israel's long-standing enemies, symbolises the believer's battle against trials, oppression, and spiritual adversity. This account encourages us that, with God's guidance, no enemy is too great, and no situation is beyond redemption: "If God is for us, who can be against us?" (Romans 8:31, KJV).

If you are facing distress, take heart in the example of David. When all seemed lost, he sought the Lord and found strength to rise again. You too can trust that God will equip you for victory. "Wait on the Lord; be strong and take heart, and wait for the Lord" (Psalm 27:14, NKJV).

Spiritual Renewal as a Precursor to Action

Before embarking on the pursuit, David's deliberate pause to seek the Lord represents a critical turning point in the narrative. Here, the emphasis is on internal strength rather than reliance solely on human resources. By "strengthening himself in the Lord," David publicly affirms that his forthcoming actions are undergirded by divine guidance. This moment is not one of mere tactical planning but of spiritual recalibration, a recognition that the true source of victory lies in alignment with God's will.

When faced with overwhelming challenges, take heart and remember that true strength does not come from sheer force but from unwavering faith. As the Bible reminds us, "Not by might, nor by power, but by My Spirit," says the Lord of Hosts" (Zechariah 4:6, NKJV). David's decision to seek strength in God was more than just preparation for battle, it was a declaration of who he was: a servant of the Lord who knew that earthly power fades without divine support. In your struggles, lean on God, for "those who hope in the Lord will renew their strength" (Isaiah 40:31, NKJV). Keep faith, for victory is not solely in your hands but in His.

The Pursuit of the Amalekites: Conflict as a Canvas for Divine Will

Subsequently, the narrative shifts from inner preparation to external action in the pursuit of the Amalekites. Authentic faith reveals itself through our actions. The Amalekites, often depicted as relentless foes of Israel, serve as a symbol of chaos and opposition to God's order.

By confronting these adversaries, David steps into a conflict that is not just strategic but profoundly spiritual. His mission symbolises the enduring battle between divine purpose and the forces that resist it.

Empowered by his renewed spirit, David's military campaign is portrayed as a divinely sanctioned undertaking. The narrative invites us to consider that the infusion of spiritual strength can transform every challenge and battle. Rather than viewing the conflict solely in terms of physical confrontation, the story encourages an understanding of warfare as a contest where moral and spiritual dimensions play a decisive role.

In Ephesians 6:12 (KJV), we read, "For we wrestle not against flesh and blood, but against principalities, against powers, against the rulers of the darkness of this world, against spiritual wickedness in high places." This verse reminds us that our real battles are not with people, but with the deeper spiritual forces of evil that influence thoughts, systems, and behaviours. Instead of fighting others, we're called to stand firm in faith, prayer, and integrity, recognising that spiritual resilience is key in times of conflict or moral challenge.

Several themes emerge from this narrative episode:

- **Divine Empowerment:** David's act of strengthening himself in the Lord underscores a central biblical teaching: true power comes from reliance on God rather than human might. His success is portrayed as inseparable from his spiritual preparedness.

- **The Interplay of Faith and Leadership:** As a leader, David models the necessity of grounding decisions and actions in a profound relationship with God. His example sets a precedent for leadership that values introspection and divine counsel over impulsive action.

- **Spiritual Meaning Behind the Conflict:** The battle against the Amalekites represents more than just a physical fight; it serves as a metaphor for the ongoing struggle against forces that oppose divine justice. This story teaches that every challenge, when faced with faith and integrity, can serve as a testament to God's guidance and protection.

Leadership Styles

In this exploration, I intend to examine two distinct leadership styles: transformational and transactional leadership. Both approaches offer unique perspectives on how leaders influence their followers, motivate others, and achieve goals. By analysing these styles, I will highlight their core principles, differences, and the impact they have on David and his men. I aim to provide a deeper understanding of how these leadership styles can be applied in various contexts, fostering both individual and collective success.

Transformational Leadership - Key Characteristics:

Transformational leaders are known for their visionary style. They clearly communicate an inspiring vision of the future that motivates others. These leaders create a supportive environment that promotes innovation, encouraging followers to think creatively and explore new ideas.

A key aspect of transformational leadership is its emphasis on personal development. These leaders are deeply invested in the growth of their team members, providing mentorship and creating a culture of intellectual stimulation. By nurturing individual initiative, they empower others to reach their full potential.

Transformational leadership is built around four key ideas. First, great leaders lead by example. They show strong values and high standards, inspiring others to follow their lead. Second, they motivate people by sharing a clear and exciting vision of the future, which helps the team feel confident and driven. Third, they encourage creativity by asking questions and getting people to think in new ways. And lastly, they treat each person as an individual, offering support and guidance based on their unique strengths and needs.

By embodying these principles, transformational leaders cultivate dynamic, forward-thinking environments that propel both personal and organisational success. Their approach enhances engagement by aligning the organisation's goals with the personal values of team members, leading to a noticeable boost in morale and commitment. This alignment fosters a sense of purpose and drives individuals to work more passionately towards shared objectives.

Additionally, transformational leaders emphasize creativity and innovation, which can spark breakthrough ideas and contribute to sustained long-term performance. This leadership style is particularly effective in fast-paced or rapidly changing environments, where adaptability and agility are crucial for success. By promoting flexibility and resilience, transformational leaders help their teams navigate change with confidence and ease.

Transactional Leadership - Key Characteristics

Transactional leadership, on the contrary, is defined by its structured, goal-oriented approach, emphasising efficiency and clear expectations. Leaders who adopt this style prioritise tasks and processes, ensuring that objectives are well-defined and accompanied by established procedures to achieve them. They maintain order by relying on a system of rewards and punishments, offering incentives to those who meet performance targets, while enforcing corrective measures for those who fall short.

Transactional leadership is a style that prioritises achieving immediate, short-term results over fostering long-term transformation. It focuses on meeting specific performance outcomes rather than cultivating sustained growth or change. This approach is especially effective in environments where consistency is crucial, established protocols must be followed, and measurable achievements are the goal.

The impact of transactional leadership is clear in several key areas. First, it creates clear expectations by precisely defining roles and responsibilities, eliminating confusion in task execution. Second, it boosts operational efficiency, particularly in settings where routine and standardised procedures are vital to maintaining high productivity.

Lastly, transactional leadership helps ensure stability in environments that require strict adherence to protocols, such as manufacturing plants or military operations, by promoting order and discipline.

Comparative Analysis, Complementary Strengths

- **Vision vs. Execution**: Transformational leaders excel at inspiring change and envisioning a better future, while transactional leaders ensure that day-to-day operations are executed efficiently.
- **Motivation vs. Accountability**: Transformational leadership motivates intrinsically by appealing to higher-order needs, whereas transactional leadership leverages extrinsic motivators like rewards and penalties to maintain performance.

- **Adaptability vs. Structure**: In uncertain or rapidly evolving situations, transformational leadership can drive innovation and adaptability. Conversely, transactional leadership provides the necessary structure and predictability in more stable, process-oriented environments.

Challenges and Limitations: Overemphasis on Vision

A leader who places too much emphasis on transformational qualities may inadvertently create an environment where vision overshadows structure. While inspiration and forward-thinking ideas are crucial, an excessive focus on the bigger picture without a solid operational framework can lead to confusion and inefficiencies. Without clear direction, team members may struggle to translate ambitious goals into actionable steps, ultimately hindering productivity and progress.

Risk of Stifling Innovation

On the other hand, an overreliance on transactional leadership can stifle creativity and dampen intrinsic motivation. When rigid structures, strict performance metrics, and routine processes dominate, employees in roles that thrive on innovation may feel constrained, demotivated and experience low morale. The pressure to meet predefined expectations can limit their willingness to take risks or explore new ideas, reducing the organisation's ability to adapt and evolve in dynamic environments.

Balancing Act

For many modern leaders, the most effective approach lies in striking a balance between transformational and transactional elements. By blending inspiration with structure, they can cultivate long-term commitment while maintaining the discipline needed to achieve short-term goals. This balance allows leaders to encourage innovation and adaptability while ensuring that day-to-day operations remain efficient and aligned with organisational objectives.

David's Leadership Style at Ziglag

David's leadership at Ziklag exemplifies a strategic blend of transformational and transactional leadership, both of which contributed to his effectiveness in guiding his followers. As a transformational leader, David inspired loyalty and resilience among his men, fostering personal growth and a shared vision even in times of adversity. His ability to instil hope and unify his followers under a common purpose reflects the core tenets of transformational leadership; motivating beyond mere exchanges to achieve long-term success.

Conversely, David also demonstrated transactional leadership by maintaining discipline, enforcing accountability, and rewarding loyalty. His fair distribution of spoils (1 Samuel 30:23-25) illustrates his commitment to structure and equitable treatment, ensuring stability and operational efficiency.

This balanced approach aligns with biblical servant leadership, as seen in Christ's example of guiding with both vision and accountability (Mark 10:45; Philippians 2:3-4). Furthermore, Proverbs 11:14 highlights the necessity of wise counsel, reinforcing David's adaptability in leadership.

By integrating transformational inspiration with transactional structure, David cultivated a leadership style that secured immediate success at Ziklag and laid the foundation for his future as king. His approach underscores the importance of leveraging multiple leadership paradigms to foster organisational strength and individual development.

Distributed leadership is a model where leadership responsibilities are shared across multiple individuals rather than concentrated in one person, promoting collaboration, empowerment, and active participation. Applied to David at Ziglad, this approach would involve empowering his team and units to take initiative and make decisions based on their expertise, fostering a culture of shared leadership.

David focused on creating an environment where his men were encouraged to take ownership, contribute, be flexible, and adapt. As we will see later, 200 men guarded the supplies while the rest fought on the front line.

The Isolating Nature of Leadership

This refers to the inherent loneliness and separateness often accompanying high-level decision-making and responsibility. Leaders can find themselves removed from their teams' day-to-day interactions, which, while sometimes necessary to maintain objectivity, can also lead to feelings of isolation and detachment.

The Roots of Isolation

Leadership carries with it the weight of responsibility, and with authority comes the burden of making difficult decisions. A leader often stands at a crossroad; faced with choices that will shape the direction of their family, ministry, team or organisation. Yet, the weight of these decisions can be isolating. The expectation to remain steadfast and certain may prevent a leader from voicing their uncertainties, for fear that doing so could weaken the confidence of those who look to them for guidance. This struggle echoes the burden of Moses, who, despite his divine calling, felt overwhelmed by the task before him. "I cannot carry all these people by myself; the burden is too heavy for me" (Numbers 11:14, NIV).

Power Dynamics: The structure of leadership creates an inherent divide. The hierarchical gap, whether subtle or pronounced, often places barriers between leaders and their teams. Colleagues may hesitate to speak openly, fearing repercussions or simply feeling the weight of formality. Meanwhile, leaders may find themselves maintaining a degree of separation, believing it necessary to uphold their authority. This distance can foster an unintended loneliness, mirroring the experience of King David, who, despite his power and following, cried out, "Turn to me and be gracious to me, for I am lonely and afflicted" (Psalm 25:16, NIV).

Emotional Vulnerability: There exists an unspoken expectation that leaders must always project confidence, regardless of their internal struggles. The pressure to maintain an image of strength can lead to an emotional façade, making it difficult to establish authentic and supportive relationships. Vulnerability may be seen as weakness, yet even Jesus, the greatest leader of all, did not shy away from expressing His anguish. In the Garden of Gethsemane, He admitted, "My soul is overwhelmed with sorrow to the point of death" (Matthew 26:38, NIV), showing that even the strongest leaders need support and connection.

Implications for Decision-Making and Well-Being

Isolation carries profound implications for both decision-making and overall well-being. When perspectives are narrowed, decision-makers find themselves trapped within an echo chamber, hearing only their own thoughts and the reinforcing voices of a select few. Without diverse input, their choices risk becoming unbalanced, lacking the wisdom that comes from a multitude of counsellors. As Proverbs 11:14 (ESV) reminds us, "Where there is no guidance, a people falls, but in an abundance of counsellors there is safety." A leader who isolates him or herself, deprives his or her decisions of the depth and insight that only a broader perspective can provide.

Beyond the realm of decision-making, prolonged isolation poses significant risks to mental health. The constant burden of solitary leadership can give rise to stress, burnout, and an overwhelming sense of loneliness. These struggles do not remain confined to the individual; they ripple outward, affecting both personal well-being and overall performance. Even Moses as mentioned, despite his strength and calling, found the weight of leadership too heavy to bear alone until his father-in-law Jethro advised him to share the load (Exodus 18:17-18). Without support and connection, the mental strain of isolation can become a formidable obstacle.

Furthermore, the fabric of trust and communication within a team begins to fray when leaders remain distant. If they withdraw from open dialogue, their team may hesitate to express concerns, voice ideas, or seek guidance. This erodes a culture of trust and collaboration, replacing it with uncertainty, low morale and disconnection.

Paul, in his letters, often emphasized the importance of mutual encouragement and communication within the body of believers, as seen in Hebrews 10:24-25 (ESV), "And let us consider how to stir up one another to love and good works, not neglecting to meet together, as is the habit of some, but encouraging one another." Just as spiritual communities thrive on connection, so too do organisations that foster care, respect, empathy, open and honest communication.

Application in Practice

1. Building a Support Network

Mentorship and Peer Groups: Actively seek out mentors and form networks with fellow leaders. Peer support groups offer a confidential space to discuss challenges and share experiences without the risk of hierarchical repercussions.

External Advisors: Consider establishing advisory boards or consulting with external experts who can offer fresh perspectives and unbiased feedback.

2. Fostering Open Communication

Transparent Dialogue: Encourage an environment where feedback flows freely in all directions. Regular one-on-one meetings and open forums can help bridge the gap between leadership and team members.

Empathy and Vulnerability: While maintaining professionalism, showing genuine concern and occasional vulnerability can 'humanize' leadership. This helps in building trust and reducing the emotional isolation that many leaders experience.

3. Delegation and Empowerment

Distribute Responsibilities: Empowering trusted team members to make decisions strengthens the team's capabilities while alleviating the weight of isolation. Delegate effectively and oversee wisely without becoming territorial: Delegate and regulate.

Cultivate Leadership within Teams: Empowering others to take on leadership roles creates a more collaborative environment and provides leaders with reliable sounding boards for ideas and concerns. There is a wise saying that 'There is no success without a successor.' Distributed leadership is a collaborative approach where leadership responsibilities are shared across individuals, promoting teamwork, autonomy, and collective decision-making.

4. Continuous Self-Reflection:

Regular Assessment: Leaders must regularly evaluate their emotional and professional well-being to maintain effectiveness and prevent burnout. Engaging in self-reflection or seeking external coaching helps them gain perspective, ensuring that isolation does not impair their decision-making or overall health.

By proactively assessing their state, leaders can identify potential stressors early, fostering resilience and sustained performance. This practice not only enhances personal well-being but also contributes to a healthier organisational environment, as a well-balanced leader is better equipped to support and inspire their team.

Take Heart

If you're feeling weary, remember that God sees your hard work and understands your exhaustion. Jesus said, "Come to me, all you who are weary and burdened, and I will give you rest" (Matthew 11:28, NIV). You're not walking this path alone.

Even Moses, a great leader, grew tired. But God sent Aaron and Hur to hold up his hands (Exodus 17:12). In the same way, lean on those around you; friends, family, and fellow believers, because "two are better than one... if either of them falls, one can help the other up" (Ecclesiastes 4:9-10, NIV).

Don't let the weight of responsibility overwhelm you. Give your worries to God, because He cares for you (1 Peter 5:7). He will renew your strength, just as He promised: "Those who hope in the Lord will renew their strength; they will soar on wings like eagles" (Isaiah 40:31, NIV).

Your work is not in vain (1 Corinthians 15:58). Keep going, stand strong, and find rest in the Lord. He will sustain you. Trust that He is working through you, and His plans for you are good.

Application: Lessons for Today

This narrative has enduring relevance, particularly in contexts of leadership and community during crises.

Shared Suffering Demands Shared Support: Just as David suffered alongside his people, modern leaders whether in business, politics, faith or community settings face challenges that are deeply personal. When disasters or setbacks occur, it is more constructive to offer support rather than to assign blame hastily.

Avoiding the Scapegoating Trap: The impulse to blame a singular leader in times of crisis can lead to fractured communities. True, the responsibility stops with leadership, nevertheless, recognising that losses often result from larger, uncontrollable forces can foster a more unified response and encourage collective problem-solving.

Embracing Vulnerability in Leadership: David's example teaches us that effective leadership does not come from a facade of invulnerability. Acknowledging one's own pain and suffering can actually build trust and solidarity among those who follow, as it humanizes the leader and reinforces the notion that everyone shares the burden. Yet it is vital to maintain dignity and a measure of confidentiality and distance to avoid familiarity and loss of respect.

The Importance of Compassionate Accountability: While accountability is crucial, it should be tempered with empathy. David's men, in their moment of crisis, failed to see that their leader was also a victim. Today, when evaluating decisions and outcomes, it is important to balance responsibility with compassion, ensuring that criticism does not deepen the wounds of those already in distress.

In summary, the chapter at Ziklag is a rich tapestry of human emotion under duress. It exposes how quickly loyalty can falter when fear and loss take hold, while simultaneously highlighting the noble qualities of steadfast leadership. Reflecting on this story invites us to examine our own responses to crises, urging us to replace blame with empathy and to stand together, even when the weight of loss seems unbearable

In the darkest moments of leadership, when the weight of responsibility grows heavy, faith-driven leaders turn to a source greater than themselves. David exemplified this when he found himself in dire straits at Ziklag. His own men, disillusioned and grieving, spoke of stoning him. Everything they held dear had been taken, their homes burned, their families captured. In that moment, David did not rely on his own strength or wisdom, he strengthened himself in the Lord.

One of the hardest lessons in leadership is understanding the fickle nature of loyalty. The same people who celebrate you today may turn against you tomorrow. David experienced this first-hand: when the people sang, *"Saul has slain his thousands, and David his ten thousand"* (1 Samuel 18:7, KJV), King Saul was jealous at this utterance and later sought his downfall. Even Jesus faced this painful reality. The crowd that shouted, *"Hosanna!"* (Matthew 21:9) as He entered Jerusalem later cried out, *"Crucify Him!"* (Luke 23:21).

A faith-driven leader does not build his or her confidence on the applause of people but on the steadfastness of their purpose. "Do not put your trust in princes, in human beings, who cannot save" (Psalm 146:3, NIV). Instead, anchor your heart in God's unwavering faithfulness. When others turn away, remember His promise: "Be strong and courageous. Do not be afraid or terrified because of them, for the Lord your God goes with you; He will never leave you nor forsake you" (Deuteronomy 31:6, NIV).

Stay faithful to your calling. Even when human loyalty wavers, God's love remains steadfast. Keep pressing forward. He who called you is faithful, and He will sustain you (1 Thessalonians 5:24).

Mission Accomplished?

David's journey also teaches us that not everyone will complete the mission with us. As he and his men pursued the Amalekites, 200 of his warriors became too exhausted to continue. David's warriors were weary because they had already endured a gruelling march before engaging in battle, both physically and emotionally drained from the intensity of their pursuit.

Their exhaustion highlights the harsh reality of endurance in leadership and warfare; some will falter along the way, unable to complete the mission despite their loyalty and willingness. The implication of their role in guarding the supplies is significant; though they did not fight in the final battle, they still played a crucial part in ensuring the success of the mission. This underscores the broader theme that every role in a mission, whether at the front lines or in support, is essential. It also reflects the importance of recognising contributions beyond direct combat, a lesson David himself later reinforced by ensuring these men received a share of the victory's spoils, emphasising fairness and unity in leadership.

Instead of shaming them, David assigned them to guard the supplies at the Besor Brook. Though they did not fight on the battlefield, their role as mentioned, remained vital to the overall victory. Similarly, Jesus left some of His disciples behind in Gethsemane while He pressed forward to fulfil His mission. A faith-driven leader recognises that not all will march the entire journey, but each person has a purpose.

Leadership rooted in faith is not about personal ambition; it is about trusting in God's guidance, embracing people's unpredictability, and recognising the value of each role in the mission. Like David, faith-driven leaders strengthen themselves in the Lord, inspiring those around them to press on, even in adversity. The journey will not always be easy; sadly, some will fall away, but through unwavering faith, victory is assured.

The Narrative of Jesus in Gethsemane

In the Garden of Gethsemane, as Jesus wrestled with the weight of His destiny, His closest disciples were asked to stay awake and keep vigil. Yet, in their human frailty, they succumbed to sleep (Matthew 26:40-41). Their absence at the critical moment is not portrayed simply as a failure but as a revealing moment of their human condition.

Their inability to remain fully present underscores the tension between divine calling and human imperfection. "And he cometh unto the disciples, and findeth them asleep, and saith unto Peter, What, could ye not watch with me one hour? Watch and pray, that ye enter not into temptation: the spirit indeed is willing, but the flesh is weak." (Matthew 26:40-41, KJV)

Even as they faltered, their earlier commitment, their presence throughout His ministry, and the very reality of their vulnerability added depth to the narrative of sacrifice and redemption. Likewise, weary leaders may find themselves burdened, feeling alone in their struggles. But take heart, Christ, who understands the depths of human weakness, remains steadfast (Hebrews 4:15-16).

God does not call the perfect; He calls the willing, sustaining them in their weakness (2 Corinthians 12:9-10). Just as Jesus restored and empowered His disciples after their failure, He strengthens those who feel weary and inadequate. Your faithfulness, even when imperfect, is seen by God, and He will complete the good work He has begun in you (Philippians 1:6). As the saying goes, 'He does not call the equipped but equips the called.'

So, to the leader who feels alone in the night watch, know this: You are not forsaken. God sees your struggle, honours your perseverance, and will refresh your spirit in due time (Isaiah 40:29-31). Stay the course, your labour in the Lord is not in vain (1 Corinthians 15:58).

Strategy at Besor

Similarly, when David left behind 200 exhausted men at Besor, we see a leader making a pragmatic decision in the midst of battle. These warriors, having given their all up to that point, were not meant to carry on the final burden of the campaign. Their fatigue did not diminish their critical role in the build up to victory; instead, their service was woven into the fabric of David's larger strategy and eventual triumph. In leaving them behind, David acknowledged the limits of human endurance and the necessity of having the right people in the right moment, even if not everyone is called to complete the final stretch.

Themes and Implications

Both narratives emphasise a central theme: the journey's success does not solely depend on every follower completing the final leg, but on the cumulative contributions of all who participated along the way. This challenges the often simplistic notion that only those who reach the finish line are significant. Instead, these stories reveal:

Human Frailty and Divine Purpose: Even in moments of weakness, the contributions of those who participate shape a larger, redemptive narrative. The disciples' failure to stay awake and the warriors' physical exhaustion highlight the very real human limitations that coexist with a divine plan. They still offered distant support.

The Value of Every Contribution: Whether or not one completes the journey, each effort is integral. The disciples and David's men both played indispensable roles in their respective missions.

Leadership and Compassion: Leaders recognise that not all are meant to bear the full burden. In making difficult decisions, like David's to leave behind those who were spent, they acknowledge individual limits and respect each person's contribution.

Application to Modern Life

These ancient narratives offer valuable lessons for our own journeys. Embracing imperfection is a crucial aspect of life, whether in our personal, professional, or spiritual pursuits. We often feel pressure to complete every endeavour perfectly, yet these stories remind us that our contributions at every stage hold significance, even if circumstances prevent us from seeing things through to the very end. The journey itself has value, and our efforts remain meaningful regardless of their perceived completeness.

Recognising different roles within any community or team is essential. Not everyone is expected to share the same responsibilities or endure the same challenges. Leaders, in particular, should appreciate that each member's participation, no matter how long or short, can be fundamental in achieving a common goal. Every role contributes to the collective success, and acknowledging this diversity fosters a more inclusive and productive environment.

Valuing the journey shifts our focus from an end-goal mindset to one that cherishes every step along the path. Rather than being solely fixated on outcomes, we learn to appreciate the process itself. Whether we are experiencing moments of triumph or struggle, our collective efforts help shape a larger purpose. Each stage of the journey offers growth, wisdom, and an opportunity to refine our understanding of success.

Grace and compassion play an equally important role in navigating life. Just as Jesus and David recognised the limitations of those around them, we too can cultivate empathy for ourselves and others. Understanding that each person's journey is unique allows us to foster a culture of support where every contribution is valued. By extending grace, we create an atmosphere of encouragement where people feel empowered to give their best without fear of judgment or inadequacy.

Embracing Humanity Along Life's Path

Life's journey is not a solitary endeavour but a shared passage, marked by moments of triumph, trials, and transitions. The stories of Jesus in Gethsemane and David at Besor call us to reconsider the significance of each step we take. These narratives remind us that while not all may complete the journey in the same way, every role played contributes to something greater than ourselves.

In Gethsemane, Jesus wrestled with the weight of His purpose, knowing that even those closest to Him would falter in his hour of need. Yet, His sacrifice was not diminished by their weakness; instead, it was made more profound by His unwavering commitment to the path laid before Him.

Similarly, at Besor, David encountered men who could go no further, physically and emotionally spent. Yet, he did not dismiss them but acknowledged their part in the greater victory. They could not fight on the front line but guarded the supplies, thus facilitating those there. The spoils of battle were shared among all, recognising that contribution is not always measured in miles travelled but in the heart invested along the way.

These stories call us to embrace our own humanity and that of those around us. There will be times when we stand strong, pressing forward with faith and determination, and times when, like those who rested at the Brook Besor (1 Samuel 30:9-10), we grow weary and must pause. Yet take heart, whether we are leading the charge or waiting by the stream, our place in God's story remains vital. He sees us, He knows our hearts, and His grace fills every gap we cannot bridge on our own (2 Corinthians 12:9).

So let us walk with compassion toward ourselves and one another. Let us honour the struggles, the quiet acts of endurance, and the unseen sacrifices that shape the path ahead. For in the kingdom of God, even the weary are not forgotten (Isaiah 40:29-31), and every step, whether bold or faltering, is held in His divine purpose.

The Bible teaches that God grants different gifts and talents to individuals for the purpose of serving others and glorifying Him. Romans 12:6–8 and 1 Corinthians 12:4–11 list gifts such as prophecy, teaching, leadership, healing, and speaking in tongues, while Ephesians 4:11–13 highlights roles like apostles, evangelists, and pastors. James 1:17 reminds us that all good gifts come from God. The Parable of the Talents (Matthew 25:14–30) emphasises using our abilities wisely rather than hiding them. Overall, Scripture encourages believers to recognise and develop their God-given gifts for the benefit of others and the growth of God's kingdom.

In the end, what truly matters is not just reaching the destination but how we walk the path, together, upheld by grace, and embracing both the struggles of humanity and the presence of the divine. As Micah 6:8 (NIV) reminds us, "He has shown you, O man, what is good. And what does the Lord require of you? To act justly and to love mercy and to walk humbly with your God."

Chapter 5:
Navigating the Journey to Victory

——————— 99 ———————

Compassion in the Midst of Loss

This chapter powerfully reflects on the transformative potential of compassion. David's choice to spare the abandoned Egyptian, as found in 1 Samuel 30: 11-15, avoiding the easy path of vengeance, resonates as a timeless lesson on the virtues of forgiveness and the redemptive strength of mercy. It challenges us to consider that sometimes, reclaiming what is lost may best be achieved not through force but through a profound act of kindness.

Strategies must be employed at critical moments of decision, where the choice between vengeance and mercy defines the outcome. Jesus broke bread with Judas, fully aware of the betrayal ahead, demonstrating a strategy of patience and divine purpose (Matthew 26:20-25, NIV).

Similarly, in Ziglag, a place scarred by past losses, David encountered a forsaken Amalekite, an Egyptian soldier. This moment demands strategic discernment. He could seek retribution, driven by his people's grief, or extend grace, recognising the power of compassion. It is in these pivotal instances, when emotions run high and stakes are great, that wisdom and intentional action can shape the future course.

Context and Setting

The ruins of Ziglag serve as a constant reminder of loss and the brutal cycle of violence. Here, David stands at a crossroads. The physical and emotional devastation of Ziglag not only underscores his personal grief but also symbolises the broader consequences of endless revenge. Within this charged atmosphere, the abandoned Egyptian emerges as an unexpected figure, a solitary presence whose vulnerability mirrors the shattered state of Ziglag itself.

The desert wind carried with it the remnants of a battle dust, echoes of pain, and the scent of uncertainty. Weary from their pursuit, David and his men pressed forward with hearts burdened yet determined. Their city, Ziklag, had been reduced to ashes by the Amalekites, and their loved ones had been taken captive. Amidst their anguish, David's faith did not waver. He sought divine guidance, and the Lord's response was clear: "Pursue, for you shall surely overtake them and without fail recover all." In other words:

'Go, Catch and Rescue!'

As they journeyed across the barren wilderness, an unexpected sight caught their attention: a lone figure collapsed under the shadow of a dying tree. An Egyptian soldier, left to perish by his Amalekite commanders, lay there in utter exhaustion. Though some of David's men saw only a burden, David saw an opportunity for compassion. Instead of striking him down in anger, as many might have in his situation, David chose to offer aid. Water and food were given, and strength slowly returned to the frail man's body.

David's decision was guided by both wisdom and mercy. Recognising the value of the Egyptian's knowledge, he chose to spare him, not merely out of compassion, but with strategic foresight. In gratitude, the man disclosed a vital truth: he had been part of the raiding party that had plundered Ziklag. More importantly, he knew the whereabouts of the Amalekites and offered to lead David to them, provided he was neither delivered back to his captors nor slain.

As Proverbs 3:21 (NIV) reminds us, "My son, do not lose sight of wisdom and discretion, for they will be life to your soul and adornment to your neck." David's discernment in this moment exemplified the power of wisdom in securing both justice and victory.

Herein lay a profound lesson: help sometimes comes from the most unexpected places. The very person abandoned as useless by the Amalekites became the key to their downfall. Had David allowed his anger to dictate his actions, he might have missed the vital information that would lead to victory.

Guided by this unexpected ally, David and his men tracked the Amalekites to their encampment. There, the enemy revelled in the spoils of their conquest, completely unaware of the storm that was about to descend upon them. But David did not act recklessly. He employed wisdom and positive leadership strategies.

Attacking at the break of dawn, he and his men took the enemy by surprise, overwhelming them in a decisive battle that raged from twilight until evening. The victory was total. Not a single hostage was lost. Every woman and child was restored to their families. The spoils of battle were claimed by David's army.

This triumph was not achieved by mere strength of arms. It was the result of faith, wisdom, and divine strategy. Victory required more than just courage. It required trust in God, kindness to the forgotten, and patience in waiting for the right moment to strike.

In life, as on the battlefield, the journey to victory is often riddled with trials. There will be moments of despair, moments when the enemy seems to have taken everything. But as David's story reveals, no defeat is final when one walks in faith. Sometimes, help will appear from the most unexpected places. The hand of divine guidance will turn even the bleakest of circumstances into an opportunity for restoration.

David's return to Ziklag would later be not just the return of a warrior, but of a leader who had chosen faith over fear, mercy over vengeance, and strategy over impulse. His journey serves as a powerful reminder that the greatest victories in life are not won by force alone but by faith in the One who goes before us, preparing the path to triumph.

Character and Conflict

David's internal conflict is at the heart of this chapter. The narrative sets up a classic confrontation between anger and mercy. Traditional expectations might dictate that one would seize the opportunity to exact vengeance and reclaim lost honour or possessions. Yet David's response is anything but predictable. Instead of allowing fury to guide his hand, he chooses compassion. This decision illuminates several key aspects of his character:

Moral Maturity: David's decision is not a mere rejection of vengeance but a testament to his profound understanding of leadership. He resists the primal urge for retribution, not out of weakness, but because he recognises that true strength lies in mercy. His choice reflects a leader who governs not by impulse, but by principle, understanding that justice and wisdom often walk hand in hand.

Emotional Complexity: Beneath David's actions lies a man wrestling with deep personal loss. His journey is not devoid of pain, yet he refuses to let sorrow harden his heart. Instead, he rises above the instinct for retaliation, offering compassion even to the most unexpected figures. His kindness toward the abandoned

Egyptian, Amalekite soldier; someone easily dismissed as insignificant, reveals a leader who balances power with humanity, embodying both the weight of grief and the grace of mercy.

Redemptive Leadership: In sparing the life of one who might have been considered an enemy, David embraces a leadership that is not built on destruction but on restoration. His choice speaks to a broader vision. One where reclaiming what has been lost does not always demand further loss. In choosing reconciliation over ruin, he demonstrates that true leadership is as much about healing as it is about victory.

Several themes emerge and resonate throughout the chapter.

Mercy Over Might

The narrative challenges the conventional association of strength with violence. David's compassion suggests that true power lies in restraint and the willingness to forgive. Meekness is not weakness, but strength under control. A professor on my doctoral programme years ago conceptualises "courageous restraint" as the capacity to remain steadfast in one's convictions while engaging respectfully and thoughtfully with opposing perspectives, without resorting to aggression or compromising fundamental values.

Joseph exemplifies mercy over might when he forgives his brothers who sold him into slavery, despite having the power to punish them as Egypt's ruler. Instead of seeking revenge, he chooses compassion, showing that true strength lies in restraint and grace. His response challenges the notion that power is demonstrated through dominance, proving instead that meekness is strength under control, guided by mercy and forgiveness.

The Possibility of Redemption

The abandoned Egyptian, a figure seemingly marooned by fate, becomes a symbol of lost potential and the possibility of renewal. David's act hints at a broader, more inclusive vision where even the outcast may be redeemed.

The Cost of Anger

By choosing mercy over vengeance, the chapter underscores the recurring cycle of violence, illustrating how retaliation often leads to an endless chain of suffering. In contrast, extending compassion has the transformative ability to disrupt this destructive pattern, fostering healing and reconciliation.

This theme resonates deeply with biblical teachings, particularly in Romans 12:19 (NIV), where Paul writes, "Do not take revenge, my dear friends, but leave room for God's wrath, for it is written: 'It is mine to avenge; I will repay,' says the Lord." This verse emphasises that vengeance belongs to God alone, encouraging believers to overcome evil with good.

Jesus' Example: Balancing Mercy and Righteous Indignation

Similarly, Jesus' instruction in Matthew 5:38-39 (NIV), "You have heard that it was said, 'Eye for eye, and tooth for tooth.' But I tell you, do not resist an evil person. If anyone slaps you on the right cheek, turn to them the other cheek also," reinforces the idea that mercy, rather than retaliation, can lead to true peace.

However, this perspective must not be taken out of context. It may be critiqued for what may seem to be idealism, as it does not seem to fully address the complexities of justice, accountability, and the potential for righteous indignation and assertiveness if forgiveness is emphasised without meaningful change or restitution.

For example, Jesus drove out the money changers in the temple, overturning their tables and declaring with fiery resolve, 'My Temple will be called a house of prayer,' but you have turned it into a den of thieves!" (Matt 21: 13, NLT). His righteous indignation burned as He defended the sanctity of His Father's house.

Thus, the chapter's message aligns with the biblical call to break the cycle of violence through love, forgiveness, and trust in divine justice.

The Power of Mercy: David's Test of Character

This chapter powerfully illustrates the theme of mercy through contrast, introspection, and symbolic imagery. Instead of allowing anger to lead to violence, David chooses an unexpected path of kindness, elevating compassion to a divine level (1 Samuel 24:10).

His internal struggle reveals a man wrestling with vengeance and the higher call of mercy, demonstrating that true strength lies not in retaliation but in self-control and trust in God's justice (Romans 12:19). The ruins of Ziglag and the abandoned Egyptian soldier serve as symbols of desolation and restoration, reinforcing the idea that even in brokenness, God provides a path to renewal (Joel 2:25).

David's choice is a lesson in faith and character. Mercy is not weakness but a reflection of God's own heart, as seen in Christ's ultimate act of grace (Luke 23:34). In moments of trial, we too are called to rise above bitterness and trust in God's sovereignty. Choosing mercy over vengeance transforms both the giver and the receiver, reminding us that justice belongs to the Lord and that He alone brings true redemption.

David's Humility and Strategic Self-Management

The Pact and Its Broader Implications

The pact between David and the wounded soldier is pivotal. It signifies more than a mere tactical alliance; it represents a reconciliation between conflicting forces. In agreeing to work together, both men acknowledge their shared humanity. The pact is a formalization of trust, a commitment that transforms an act of desperation into a strategic manoeuvre.

The soldier's intimate knowledge of the terrain and enemy movements becomes the key that unlocks the path to the raiding party. Through this alliance, David not only averts immediate danger but also sets a precedent for embracing diversity of thought and experience within his ranks.

Help From Unexpected Places

At its heart, this chapter reflects on the unpredictability of aid and the humility required to receive it. As mentioned, help often comes from the most unexpected sources in moments of crisis. David's acceptance of assistance from someone once deemed an enemy underscores the power of open-mindedness and adaptability.

This theme resonates with the story of Naaman (2 Kings 5:1-14), who, despite his initial pride, found healing only after surrendering to an unassuming remedy, dipping seven times in the muddy waters of the Jordan. At first, he resisted, expecting a grander cure, but his eventual obedience led to restoration. His journey mirrors the broader truth that the solutions we resist, or even scorn, may hold the very redemption we seek.

Both narratives remind us that when we let go of our preconceptions, we open ourselves to transformation, whether through unexpected allies or unlikely means. However, this surrender can be painfully difficult when our will conflicts with God's purpose, challenging us to trust in His greater plan.

Lessons in Humility and Leadership

This section masterfully weaves themes of vulnerability, trust, and redemption. David's transformation, marked by his ability to put aside anger and form a pact with a wounded adversary, undoubtedly demonstrates exemplary self-management. By accepting help from an unlikely source, he not only safeguards his men but also illustrates that true leadership lies in the willingness to learn, adapt, and embrace the unexpected. This experience therefore, stands as a powerful narrative on the virtues of humility and the enduring strength found in unity, even when it comes from those we might least expect.

Your most significant victories in life will often require a combination of unwavering faith, divine wisdom, and a God-given strategy. Challenges may arise that seem insurmountable, but through trust in God, seeking His guidance, and applying His wisdom, you can overcome any obstacle.

Faith: Faith is the foundation of all victories in our lives as Believers. Hebrews 11:6 (NIV) reminds us, "And without faith it is impossible to please God, because anyone who comes to him must believe that he exists and that he rewards those who earnestly seek him." Just as David trusted in the Lord when facing Goliath (1 Samuel 17:45-47), we too must stand in faith, believing that God will fight for us.

Wisdom: Godly wisdom directs our steps and prevents us from making decisions based on fear or human reasoning. James 1:5 (NIV) encourages us, "If any of you lacks wisdom, you should ask God, who gives generously to all without finding fault, and it will be given to you." When King Solomon faced the daunting task of ruling Israel, he asked God for wisdom rather than riches or power (1 Kings 3:9-12), and as a result, he became one of the greatest kings in history. Likewise, we should seek divine wisdom in every situation.

Divine Strategy: Victory often requires a God-ordained strategy rather than relying on our own strength. Joshua and the Israelites conquered Jericho not through military might but by obeying God's unusual battle plan, marching around the walls for seven days and then shouting in faith (Joshua 6:2-5, 20). This teaches us that when we submit to God's plan, even when it doesn't make sense to us, He brings about miraculous breakthroughs.

Real-Life Application:

Imagine facing a career setback, a broken relationship, or a financial crisis. Instead of reacting with panic or despair, you can apply these exact principles of:

Faith: "Trust in the Lord with all thine heart" (Proverbs 3:5) reminds us to rely fully on God's wisdom rather than our own understanding. When we trust Him completely, we can rest in the promise of Romans 8:28 *"And we know that all things work together for good to them that love God, to them who are the called according to his purpose."* Even when life seems uncertain or difficult, God is orchestrating everything for our ultimate good. Faith in His plan allows us to walk in peace, knowing He is in control.

Wisdom: Before making decisions, turn to prayer, Scripture, and wise mentors for guidance. Proverbs 3:5-6 reminds us to trust in the Lord completely rather than relying on our own understanding, and He will lead us in the right direction. James 1:5 reassures us that if we ask God for wisdom, He will generously provide it.

Proverbs 15:22 emphasises the importance of seeking counsel, noting that plans fail without guidance but succeed with the input of many advisers.

Additionally, Psalm 32:8 assures us that God will instruct and guide us with His loving counsel. By seeking wisdom from Him and trusted mentors, we can make choices that align with His will.

Divine Strategy: Be sensitive to the Holy Spirit's leading. Sometimes, God may direct you to take a bold step, like Joshua leading Israel around Jericho in silence before the walls fell (Joshua 6:2-5). At other times, He may call you to wait patiently, as David did when he refused to take Saul's life, trusting in God's perfect timing (1 Samuel 24:6-7).

And in some situations, His strategy may seem unusual, like Jesus telling Peter to find tax money in a fish's mouth (Matthew 17:27). No matter the approach, trust that "the steps of a good man are ordered by the Lord" (Psalm 37:23), and He will guide you in His perfect wisdom.

When you align your faith, wisdom, and strategy with God's will, you position yourself for victory that glorifies Him and strengthens your testimony.

Your greatest victories require faith, wisdom, and a divine strategy. The story of David at Ziglag stands as a timeless testament to this truth. David's unwavering faith became his beacon. He believed that even in defeat, there was a higher plan at work; a divine strategy waiting to be revealed.

David's response was not one of immediate retaliation driven by anger or impulse. Instead, he took a step back to seek wisdom. In the silence of his heart, he listened for guidance beyond his own understanding. It was this wisdom that transformed a seemingly hopeless situation into an opportunity for redemption. David knew that victory was not merely about reclaiming what was lost but about restoring hope and honour.

With strategic deliberation and trust in the divine, he set out to gather intelligence on the enemy. His measured approach was a stark contrast to the chaos of the initial attack, demonstrating that victory is often born from thoughtful planning and a reliance on something greater than human strength.

As the narrative unfolded, David's actions painted a vivid picture of a leader who trusted in God's plan. With each calculated move, his faith provided the courage to face formidable odds, and his wisdom allowed him to see the hidden patterns in the enemy's strategy.

The divine strategy was not an abstract concept but a clear path revealed through prayer, reflection, and courageous action. When David finally struck back, it was with the full force of a well-prepared plan. A plan that not only reclaimed what was lost but also re-established the spirit and unity of his people.

This story reminds us that our greatest victories, whether spiritual, emotional, personal, or professional, are not won by our strength alone but through faith, wisdom, divine strategy, and trust in God's purpose. Just as David sought the Lord at Ziklag (1 Samuel 30:6-8), finding strength and guidance in his darkest hour, we too can lean on God's direction. Even in our most challenging moments, He shapes our path toward greater triumph.

Chapter 6:
Divine Restoration and Victory

———————— 99 ————————

The account of David's decisive victory over the Amalekites is not just a historical triumph. It is a powerful lesson in leadership, resilience, and divine providence; one of hope after despair. David and his men, driven by urgency and faith, struck their enemies at their most vulnerable, while they indulged in complacency. This strategic ambush was not merely a display of military prowess but a testament to the wisdom of preparation and the power of divine intervention.

The battle reveals a powerful truth: true strength must be guided by both vigilance and faith. David remained watchful, sought God's direction with unwavering belief, and acted with boldness. His victory wasn't simply a result of physical might, it stemmed from courage, wisdom, and deep dependence on divine guidance. His leadership shone through in the way he inspired his men, chased down his enemies, and recovered all that had been taken. It was a blend of strategic thinking and steadfast trust in God.

This victory reminds us that setbacks are not defeats but divine setups for restoration. In life there will be moments of loss and despair, yet those who persevere with faith will reclaim what was taken. As Scripture declares, "But thanks be to God! He gives us the victory through our Lord Jesus Christ" (1 Corinthians 15:57, NIV).

David's victory over the Amalekites inspires us to face our own battles, both external challenges and inner struggles with wisdom, faith, and bold determination. For example, when at last the pursuit led them to the enemy's encampment, the battle that ensued was not one fought solely with the clashing of swords or the thunder of arrows. It was a battle waged on two fronts: the physical and the spiritual. David's forces, driven by a mixture of righteous anger and divine assurance, engaged the Amalekites with a fervour that transcended ordinary warfare.

The ensuing victory was swift and complete. The captives were rescued and the spoils of the raid were restored. Yet, more importantly, the battle reaffirmed a timeless truth: that divine guidance, when sought with a sincere heart, is capable of transforming despair into deliverance. Victory belongs to those who refuse to surrender to defeat, who listen for divine direction, and who march forward with purpose, reclaiming hope after and over despair.

This passage carries profound spiritual significance and practical real-life applications, particularly in the areas of faith, vigilance, and strategic action. Let's break it down:

Victory Through Readiness and Divine Timing

David's triumph was not merely a display of military strength. It was a testament to the power of seizing the right moment. His victory was not won by sheer force alone, but by a readiness that had been forged through faith and discipline. In our lives today this same principle holds true. True preparedness is not just about physical readiness but about being spiritually attuned, poised to act when God presents an opportunity.

Scripture repeatedly calls for such vigilance. "Be dressed ready for service and keep your lamps burning," Jesus exhorts in Luke 12:35

(NIV), reminding His followers that readiness is an essential part of faith. It is not enough to trust in God's timing. We must also be prepared to move when He calls.

David and his men understood this well. While their enemies, the Amalekites, revelled in overconfidence, indulging in feasting and celebration, David's warriors remained watchful. Their alertness led to victory, proving that complacency in moments of comfort can be a greater threat than the fiercest of battles. Likewise, we must resist the temptation to grow spiritually lax in seasons of ease. True faith is not only about standing firm in hardship but also about staying vigilant in times of success, ever ready for the doors God may open.

The Perils of Complacency

The Amalekites believed themselves to be untouchable, their confidence resting on a fragile illusion of security. Yet, beneath the surface of their perceived strength lay the seeds of their downfall. Blinded by arrogance, they failed to recognise the danger creeping ever closer.

History has shown that when people indulge in sin or revel too deeply in their successes, they unknowingly expose themselves to ruin. Their guard lowers, their vision narrows, and they become easy prey to the very forces they once dismissed. Proverbs 16:18 (NIV) offers a timeless warning: "Pride goes before destruction, a haughty spirit before a fall."

So it was with the Amalekites. Their overindulgence bred complacency, their distractions dulled their awareness, and their lack of spiritual vigilance left them defenceless. In the end, what they had presumed to be their moment of triumph became the stage for their greatest defeat.

God Turns Defeat into Victory

What appeared to be a certain defeat: David's camp destroyed and families captured, was turned around because he sought direction from God (1 Samuel 30:8), and responded with boldness, despite the overwhelming adversity, despair, and opposition he faced.

This reminds us that no situation is beyond redemption. With faith and strategic obedience, setbacks can become setups for greater comebacks.

Application for us Today

In the journey of life, opportunities often present themselves to those who are prepared. Just as David and his men were always ready for battle and attuned to God's guidance, we too must cultivate our skills, faith, and discipline so that when the right moment arrives, we can act decisively. In 1 Samuel 30, David and his men returned to Ziklag only to find it burned and their families taken captive. Though grief-stricken, David did not succumb to despair.

Instead, he sought God's direction and pursued his enemies, ultimately recovering all that had been lost. His readiness allowed him to act swiftly and effectively. Likewise, in our careers, relationships, and spiritual journeys, preparedness is the foundation of success. Those who cultivate wisdom and diligence position themselves to seize life's defining moments.

As we pursue success, we must remain cautious against arrogance and distraction. The Amalekites, indulging in their stolen riches, grew complacent and failed to secure their stronghold. Their carelessness led to their downfall when David and his men reclaimed what had been taken. This illustrates the dangers of unchecked pride and neglect. James 4:6 (NIV) reminds us, "God opposes the proud but gives grace to the humble."

Whether in business, finances, or spiritual growth, humility and vigilance are essential to avoiding unexpected setbacks. Just as a wise steward protects his assets, we must guard our hearts and efforts against the dangers of complacency.

Yet, even when life brings hardship, setbacks need not be permanent. David's response to the devastation of Ziklag exemplifies resilience and faith. Rather than being paralysed by loss, he turned to God for guidance, demonstrating the power of seeking divine direction in times of trouble. God assured him of victory, and he recovered all that was taken through obedience and decisive action.

This narrative underscores the biblical principle that our failures and losses can become stepping stones to greater victories. Romans 8:28 reassures us that "in all things God works for the good of those who love Him." Instead of allowing setbacks to define us, we should trust God's plan, take bold steps toward restoration, and emerge stronger than before.

Ultimately, life's trials and triumphs serve to shape us. By staying prepared, remaining humble, and trusting God in adversity, we align ourselves with His purpose. David's story is not just one of recovery but of faith in action, a reminder that, through God's guidance, we can turn every trial into triumph, messes into messages, muddles into miracles, stumbling blocks into stepping stones, obstacles into opportunities and scars into stars.

God's Promise of Restoration

The story of David echoes a prophetic promise found in Joel 2:25, where God declares, "I will restore to you the years that the swarming locust has eaten, the crawling locust, the consuming locust, and the chewing locust." These creatures symbolise physical devastation and the erosion of time, opportunities, and joy; elements that trials, setbacks, and spiritual opposition often strip away.

David's life was marked by seasons of significant loss and hardship. He endured betrayal, exile, and the seeming destruction of his destiny. At times, the anointing on his life seemed like a distant promise rather than a present reality. Yet, despite the years consumed by turmoil, God was faithful in restoring him, placing him on the throne of Israel and fulfilling His word.

This biblical principle reveals an unshakable truth: no loss is beyond God's redemption. Even when life's circumstances, our own failures, or the enemy's attacks seem to rob us of time and purpose, God's restorative power remains at work. What was stolen will not only be returned but often multiplied in ways we could never imagine.

A Word of Encouragement: You Will Make it Safely Through

In my book, *Safely Through on Broken Pieces*, I share a message of hope, resilience, and faith in the midst of life's storms. Life does not always go as planned. Sometimes, we experience loss, setbacks, and moments where it feels as if everything around us is falling apart. But even in brokenness, there is hope. Let us consider Paul:

The story of Paul's shipwreck in Acts 27 powerfully reminds us that even when disaster strikes, God still has a way of bringing us safely through. The ship was destroyed, yet Paul and the 275 others reached the shore, not on a whole vessel but on broken pieces. This is the heart of the message: We do not need to have everything intact to make it to where God is leading us. What we have left is enough.

We often dwell on what we have lost rather than appreciating what still remains. In our sorrow over brokenness, we sometimes forget that even shattered pieces can still serve a purpose. God does not require perfection to fulfil His plans. What may seem like a hopelessly damaged dream or an irreparable situation can become the very tool He uses to create a renewed and beautiful future.

A powerful reminder and example of this is found in the story of Joseph (Genesis 50:20). After being betrayed by his brothers and sold into slavery, Joseph endured years of hardship. Yet, despite the brokenness of his past, God used those very circumstances to elevate him to a position where he could save many lives. As Joseph told his brothers, "You intended to harm me, but God intended it for good to accomplish what is now being done, the saving of many lives." (Genesis 50:20, NIV). This reminds us that even in our brokenness, God is still at work, shaping a greater purpose.

Brokenness does not mean defeat. It is easy to assume that when things fall apart, the story is over. But time and time again, scripture shows us that God brings restoration through broken things. A seed must break open to grow into a tree. A grain of wheat must be crushed to make bread. Even Jesus allowed Himself to be broken so that through Him, we could be made whole. Our broken places are not the end of our journey; they are simply part of the process of transformation.

Storms come with purpose, even when we cannot immediately see it. Paul did not set out to be shipwrecked, yet that very storm positioned him for the next chapter of his mission. In the same way, the difficulties we endure often lead us to places we never expected, places where our faith is strengthened, our purpose is clarified, and our trust in God deepens.

If you find yourself in a season where the waters are rough and the vessel you once depended on is no longer holding together, take heart. You may not have everything you started with, but what you have left is enough. Even if all you have are broken pieces, they are still capable of carrying you forward. Hope remains. Your story is not over. And just like Paul and his companions, you will make it safely to shore; even on broken pieces using what you have left, not on what you have lost though many and precious.

If you feel like time has been wasted, like opportunities have slipped through your fingers, or that life's trials have left you broken, take heart. The same God who restored David's years and fulfilled His promise to him is still in the business of restoration today.

He can take the broken pieces of your past and use them as a testimony of His faithfulness.

As Isaiah 61:7 (NKJV) proclaims, "Instead of your shame you shall have double honour, and instead of confusion they shall rejoice in their portion. Therefore, in their land they shall possess double; everlasting joy shall be theirs." No pain, delay, or loss is outside His power to redeem. Trust in His timing, hold fast to His promises, and watch as He restores what was lost and gives even greater than before.

The Unshakable Promise of God's Restoration

Dear friend, take heart! The story of David's recovery and God's promise to restore the years the enemy has stolen (Joel 2:25) are not just historical accounts; they are living testimonies of God's faithfulness to you today.

When life's battles leave you weary, losses seem overwhelming, and it feels as if time and trials have taken too much, know this: God is not finished with your story. His plan is not just to return what was lost but to restore you completely: body, soul, and spirit.

The Lord declares that you will recover all (1 Samuel 30:8), not just in material blessings but in peace, purpose, joy, and strength. Even in the darkest moments, His justice and mercy are working on your behalf. Hold fast to hope, for what was stolen will be redeemed, what was broken will be healed, and what was lost will be found. Trust in the God who makes all things new! (Revelation 21:5).

A Call to Faith and Resilience

The stories of restoration compel us to reframe our experiences of loss. They encourage us to view setbacks as opportunities for growth, where every reclaimed possession or recovered year is a testament to God's enduring faithfulness. The narrative arc from loss to recovery mirrors our own journeys of healing and redemption; each personal trial, when met with faith, can be transformed into a chapter of victory. David's victory over the Amalekites becomes a symbolic rallying cry: no force of destruction, no enemy's design, is too great for God's restorative power.

Simply put, the message that "God restores everything we lost" is a timeless beacon of hope. Whether it is the physical reclamation of stolen treasures or the spiritual recovery of lost time and joy, these narratives affirm that with God, every loss is 'temporary', and every setback can be transformed into a profound testimony of renewal. Embracing this promise allows us to navigate life's adversities with unwavering faith, confident that what has been taken will be returned in fulness, and that our story, like David's, is one of ultimate redemption.

Biblical Context

In the Book of Job, Job endures profound loss and suffering. Despite his pain, he remains faithful to God. In Job 42:10, after Job intercedes for his friends, God restores his fortunes, doubling what he once had. This act of restoration is not only about material or social abundance; it's a powerful testimony to God's grace and sovereignty. The doubling signifies that God's blessings far exceed the losses incurred, affirming that no pain or setback is wasted in the divine scheme of things.

Double for Your Trouble

If you are feeling broken-hearted, take heart; your pain is not the end of your story. Just as Job endured unimaginable loss but was later restored with twice as much as he had before (Job 42:10), God is able to turn your sorrow into joy and give you double for your trouble. He sees your tears, hears your cries, and promises beauty for ashes. Isaiah 61:3 (NIV) reminds us that God gives "a crown of beauty instead of ashes, the oil of joy instead of mourning, and a garment of praise instead of a spirit of despair." Hold on, your restoration is coming, and it will be greater than you ever imagined!

Divine Justice and Mercy: The promise to "double" what was lost highlights the interplay of divine justice and mercy. It reassures us that God notices every hardship and, in His perfect timing, provides a reward that is even greater than what was taken away. This reflects a deep truth in biblical theology: God redeems suffering and transforms trials into testimonies of His enduring love.

Encouragement to Endure

The verse in Isaiah 61:1 serves as a motivation to endure through life's storms. It teaches that suffering, though painful, is not the final chapter. Instead, it is a part of the journey that prepares us for a richer future, both materially, emotionally and spiritually. We are encouraged to hold onto our faith even in the midst of loss, trusting that God's plan involves restoration that surpasses our current understanding.

A Call to Action

"Go take it back" is a powerful call to action, urging us to actively reclaim what has been lost. It challenges us to move beyond passive waiting and step boldly into the fullness of God's promises. What have you surrendered that God is calling you to reclaim? Where in your life have you accepted loss when restoration is within reach?

This is not just about hoping, it's about aligning your heart, faith, and actions with the truth that God's power is already at work. He specializes in turning sorrow into joy, setbacks into setups for blessing. Will you take the step? Hope is not distant. It's waiting for you to take hold of it.

Application to Believers: Restoration Beyond Material Gains

While Job's restoration involved tangible blessings, the principle applies to every aspect of life: emotional, relational, spiritual among others. When facing loss, disappointment, or failure, the promise is that God is capable of restoring every area of our lives. Whether it's broken relationships, lost opportunities, or diminished hope, we are invited to trust that God can not only mend, but multiply what was lost.

Claiming Your Inheritance

The directive "Go Take it Back!" reminds us that restoration is a proactive pursuit. It challenges us to step out in faith, actively seek God's promises, and refuse to accept defeat. It is about reclaiming what was lost and embracing the fullness of life that God intends, a life marked by resilience, hope, and extraordinary blessing.

"Double for Your Trouble"— A Divine Promise of Restoration

Life's trials often leave us feeling broken, lost, and uncertain about the future. Yet, within the pages of Scripture, God reveals a profound truth: suffering is never the final chapter. The story of Job, as already mentioned, stands as a testament to this promise, an assurance that God's restoration is not just about regaining what was lost but about receiving an even greater measure of blessing.

This powerful verse is worth repeating: "Instead of your shame you will receive a double portion, and instead of disgrace you will rejoice in your inheritance. And so you will inherit a double portion in your land, and everlasting joy will be yours." (Isaiah 61:7, NIV)

The Test of Faith and the Triumph of Restoration

As we see earlier, Job's journey was one of immense loss: his wealth, health, and even his children were taken from him. Yet, in the depths of his suffering, he held onto his integrity and trust in God. His friends doubted, his wife despaired, but Job remained steadfast. And in the end, Scripture declares: "The Lord restored his fortunes and gave him twice as much as he had before." (Job 42:10, NIV)

Another case in point already mentioned but repeated here for emphasis is that of Joseph who was betrayed by his brothers, sold into slavery, falsely accused, and imprisoned. Yet, through every hardship, he remained faithful to God. In time, he was elevated to the highest position in Egypt; from the pit to the prison to the palace, under Pharaoh and was able to save his family from famine (Genesis 41:39-41; Genesis 50:20). Use your favour against your famine.

This is not just a historical account but a spiritual principle. When we endure trials with faith, we position ourselves for divine restoration. What the enemy intended for harm, God transforms into a testimony of His faithfulness (Genesis 50:20; Romans 8:28).

Endurance Through the Storm

Suffering often tempts us to question God's plan, but the refining fire of trials is where faith is tested and strengthened. James reminds us: "Blessed is the one who perseveres under trial because, having stood the test, that person will receive the crown of life that the Lord has promised to those who love him." James 1:12, (NIV).

Endurance is the bridge between loss and restoration, a powerful testament to faith and resilience. When we trust God in our pain, we surrender our struggles to His greater plan, allowing Him to work behind the scenes in ways we cannot yet see. Even in our darkest moments, He is preparing a blessing beyond our expectations, shaping beauty from brokenness, purpose from problems, opportunities from obstacles, stepping stones from stumbling blocks, messages from messes, testimonies from tests and triumphs from trials.

Let us consider Ruth's faithfulness, despite losing everything, led her to a new beginning and a place in the lineage of Christ (Ruth 4:13-17). Furthermore, Esther, though facing great danger, trusted God's timing and was used to save her people (Esther 4:14). So hold on, stay strong, and keep moving forward, knowing that every challenge endured with faith brings you closer to the restoration and joy He has in store.

Claiming the Promise of Abundance

God's nature is abundant, not only in material blessings but also in peace, joy, and spiritual renewal. Jesus affirms this in John 10:10 (NIV): "I have come that they may have life, and have it to the full."

Moreover, 3 John 1:2 (KJV) declares, "Beloved, I wish above all things that thou mayest prosper and be in health, even as thy soul prospereth." God's provision and prosperity are evident throughout Scripture. In Philippians 4:19 (NKJV), we are assured, "And my God shall supply all your need according to His riches in glory by Christ Jesus." This promise reminds us that His abundance is not limited to what we see but extends to every area of our lives, ensuring that we lack nothing as we trust in Him.

Hold On, Your Double Portion is Coming

I cannot emphasise enough that there is a setup for a greater comeback in every setback. God does not leave His children in despair; He turns mourning into dancing (Psalm 30:11), ashes into beauty (Isaiah 61:3), and trials into testimonies (Romans 8:28). If you are in a season of hardship, take heart. The God who restored Job (Job 42:10), Joseph (Genesis 50:20), Ruth (Ruth 4:13-17), Esther (Esther 8:1-17), and many others will restore you. "Weeping may endure for a night, but joy comes in the morning." (Psalm 30:5, KJV)

Hold onto your faith, keep pressing forward, and be prepared, your double portion is on its way.

Chapter 7:
Managing Success Effectively

———— 99 ————

The sun dipped below the horizon as David and his weary men pressed on. Their bodies ached from the relentless pursuit, but their spirits surged with renewed vigour. The promise of divine restoration was near, and they clung to God's faithfulness like warriors gripping their swords as they crested the final hill; the sight before them sent a wave of holy determination through their ranks.

Below, the Amalekites revelled in drunken celebration. Fires burned bright, illuminating their plunder: David's possessions, the families of his men, and every precious thing stolen from Ziklag. The enemy, convinced of their victory, had let their guard down. They were unaware that a greater force was about to descend upon them, one empowered by human strength and the hand of the Almighty.

With a nod from David, the men spread out, forming a strategic assault. The command was given, and they swept through the Amalekite camp like a storm. Swords clashed, arrows flew, and cries of terror erupted from the enemy ranks. The battle raged under the vast canopy of the night, but there was no contest. David's men were instruments of divine justice. The victory was absolute. The Amalekites lay defeated, and not a single thing was lost.

David stood among the restored belongings, his breath heavy but his heart light. God had done what He promised: *complete restoration*. God's command was: 'Go, Catch and Rescue!' The same God who assured His people through the prophet Joel, *"I will restore to you the years that the locusts have eaten"* (Joel 2:25, NKJV), had proven His word true once again.

Every wife, child, possession, and livestock was accounted for. Nothing was missing. Not only had they recovered their own, but they also took back the spoils of war, gaining more than they had before. It was double for their trouble; a fulfilment of God's principle as seen in Job's life: *"The Lord restored his fortunes and gave him twice as much as he had before"* (Job 42:10, NIV).

David's men, exhausted yet victorious, looked to their leader with reverence. They no longer thought of stoning their leader. This was not just a battle won; it was a divine demonstration that no setback was final when God was involved. His grace was sufficient, even in the midst of devastation.

As David gathered his people and they lifted praises to the Lord, he knew this was more than a physical restoration; it was a spiritual renewal. Through trial and tribulation, they had learned a fundamental truth: God's promises do not fail. When He declares restoration, He brings it to pass completely, abundantly, and in His perfect timing. "If it had not been the Lord who was on our side, now may Israel say; If it had not been the Lord who was on our side, when men rose against us. Then they had swallowed us up quick, when their wrath was kindled against us:" Psalm 124:1-3 (KJV)

The fires of Ziklag had once reduced their home to ashes, but now, a greater fire burned within their hearts, the fire of faith, emboldened by victory and sustained by divine grace.

Managing Success with Humility and Generosity

David stood before his men, the weight of leadership heavy on his shoulders. Victory had been won, but now a different test emerged, the fair distribution of the spoils. Among his warriors were 200 men who had remained behind, not out of weakness, but out of exhaustion and necessity. They had guarded the supplies, ensuring the strength and stability of the entire force.

Some among the fighters argued that these men did not deserve a share, but David saw things differently. He understood that every role in God's plan has purpose and value. Just as a body functions through many parts (1 Corinthians 12:12-27), so too does a community thrive when each person fulfils his or her duty.

Rather than giving in to division, David stood firm in justice and wisdom. He declared that all would share alike, whether they fought on the battlefield or safeguarded the camp (1 Samuel 30:24-25). This was not just military strategy; it was a reflection of God's righteousness. Jesus illustrated a similar principle in the parable of the workers in the vineyard (Matthew 20:1-16). Though some labourers worked all day and others joined only in the final hours, the master paid them all the same wage, emphasising God's grace and sovereignty in rewarding faithfulness, not just effort.

In our lives, we must recognise the value of every role, whether seen or unseen. Just as David honoured all of their contributions, we are called to appreciate the efforts of those who serve in different capacities. Victory is not just for the ones in the spotlight, but for all who faithfully play their part. Let us be encouraged to see God's hand in every task, knowing He rewards faithfulness in all things.

In the grand design of God's plan, every person has a role, whether standing on the battlefield or securing the camp. Just as David declared that those who stayed behind to guard the supplies would share in the victory (1 Samuel 30:24), we are reminded that no contribution is insignificant in God's eyes. It is easy to judge others based on visible effort, but God looks at the heart, not appearances. Take heart, your faithfulness, even in unseen places, is valued by the Lord, and He rewards those who serve Him with a sincere heart.

This verse sums it up well: "But the Lord said to Samuel, 'Do not consider his appearance or his height, for I have rejected him. The Lord does not look at the things people look at. People look at the outward appearance, but the Lord looks at the heart.'" (1 Samuel 16:7 NIV).

Some may be called to lead, fight, or sacrifice in ways that seem grand, while others serve quietly in the background, both are equally vital. This challenges us to honour all roles and resist pride or envy. Instead of seeking recognition, let us trust that God sees and rewards faithfulness, no matter how unseen by human eyes. Will you embrace your calling, knowing that God values every act of obedience?

Critical Principles About Leadership

David's decision reveals critical principles about leadership, fairness, and recognising the value of every individual in God's plan. As mentioned above, the men who stayed behind were not lazy or weak; they played a necessary role in guarding supplies and ensuring the mission's success. This highlights a fundamental truth: not all contributions are visible, but all are valuable.

Let us consider and summarise some further themes and application we can glean from their experience:

1. **A Just and Generous Leader:** David's response demonstrates humility and generosity. He acknowledged

that success comes from God and, as such should not be hoarded but shared. His actions set an example of servant leadership, recognising that every role in the community matters.

2. **God's Perspective on Effort and Role:** Human judgment often elevates visible effort over unseen contributions. However, God values faithfulness in every role. Just as the 200 men were vital in securing the camp, we must recognise that every public or private calling is important in God's kingdom.

3. **Unity and Fairness in God's Community:** David's decision to share the spoils equally prevented division among his people. It reinforced the principle that the community thrives when all are treated with fairness and respect. In the church and broader society, this lesson remains relevant: success should be shared, and contributions should be recognised, regardless of how visible they are.

However, this could be seen as promoting a noble ideal. In reality, both in the church and broader society, success is frequently tied to visibility, status, or measurable outcomes. Often, unseen contributions (like emotional labour, behind-the-scenes support, prayer, or marginalised voices) are not properly acknowledged.

Yet, it is also important to balance fairness with responsibility. Scripture warns against idleness and slothfulness. Paul writes, "If anyone is not willing to work, let him not eat" (2 Thessalonians 3:10, ESV), emphasizing that communal provision does not excuse laziness. Proverbs similarly cautions, "The soul of the sluggard craves and gets nothing, while the soul of the diligent is richly supplied" (Proverbs 13:4, ESV). David's act was not an endorsement of sloth, but a recognition of the interconnected roles within the community. A just community supports each member, but also calls each one to diligent participation.

Assessing Effort – A Christ-like Perspective

In Leadership

True leadership goes beyond mere authority; it requires the ability to recognise and appreciate the value of every role within a team or organisation. Just as a body is made up of many parts, each with its own function, so too is a community of individuals working together. A leader must foster unity rather than division, ensuring that no contribution is overlooked. The Apostle Paul reminds us in 1 Corinthians 12:12-26 that every part of the body is essential, no matter how small or unseen it may seem. Therefore, leading with humility and gratitude means acknowledging and affirming the efforts of every individual, recognising that their contributions are vital to the whole.

In Daily Life

Whether in the workplace, ministry, or family, it is easy to focus on visible accomplishments while overlooking the quiet, unseen acts of service that sustain everything around us. Yet these hidden efforts are just as important as those that receive recognition. Scripture encourages us in Colossians 3:23-24 to work wholeheartedly, not for human approval, but as an offering to the Lord, who sees all. Even when no one else notices, God is aware of our faithfulness and will reward us in His perfect time.

In Spiritual Growth

We often measure others by what they do or how they appear, but God sees far beyond that. In Jeremiah 17:10 (NIV), He declares, "I the Lord search the heart and examine the mind, to reward each person according to their conduct, according to what their deeds deserve." Unlike humans, who focus on outward behaviour, God discerns the true motives behind every action. Instead of making assumptions based on what is visible, let's ask Him for the wisdom to see people through His eyes, with grace, understanding, and a heart that values sincerity over mere appearances.

Ethical Implications of Generosity in Leadership: Faithfulness Over Visibility

The Bible presents generosity as a defining characteristic of godly leadership, exemplified not only in David's actions but also in the lives of leaders like Moses and Nehemiah. Proverbs 11:25 (NIV) declares, "A generous person will prosper; whoever refreshes others will be refreshed." This principle extends beyond material giving to an entire leadership ethos focused on the well-being of others.

Moses, despite personal reluctance, led the Israelites with a sacrificial spirit, interceding on their behalf even when they rebelled (Exodus 32:11-14). His leadership demonstrates that true authority is exercised for the benefit of the people, not personal gain. Nehemiah, too, exemplifies this principle, choosing not to burden the people with taxes and instead devoting his own resources to rebuild Jerusalem (Nehemiah 5:14-19). These examples reinforce the idea that leadership is a stewardship, not a platform for self-promotion.

Such an ethical perspective challenges modern leadership paradigms that equate success with individual achievement, wealth, entitlement or power. Leaders today, whether in business, politics, or ministry, must ask themselves: Are they using their influence for personal advancement, or to uplift others? True biblical leadership calls for generosity in action, humility in service, and a commitment to justice. It is not merely about giving but about fostering a culture of trust, responsibility, and shared flourishing.

Leaders who embrace this calling will not only impact those they serve but will also find that generosity in God's economy leads to lasting spiritual and communal prosperity. How will you lead?

Will you choose faithfulness over fame? Organisations, ministries, communities, and leaders who prioritise steadfast commitment over visibility shape a culture where contribution matters more than status. The biblical model of shared rewards reminds us that every role is vital, proving that true significance is not measured by public recognition but by unwavering service. Step up, lead with faithfulness, and transform the culture around you!

The challenge is clear: In today's world, success is often tied to status and personal achievement. But true success isn't just about what we gain, it's about how we handle it. Will we cling to our blessings for ourselves, or will we steward them with humility and generosity? Can you stand to be blessed? Can you handle success and remain humble, empathetic, and grounded when you reach the heights of success?

The Test of Blessing

Many people pray for blessings, but few consider the responsibility that comes with them. The Bible warns us about the dangers of forgetting where we came from when we experience abundance.

Deuteronomy 8:11-18 (NIV) reminds us: "Be careful that you do not forget the Lord your God, failing to observe his commands, his laws and his decrees… Otherwise, when you eat and are satisfied, when you build fine houses and settle down… then your heart will become proud and you will forget the Lord your God, who brought you out of Egypt, out of the land of slavery."

Success, if not stewarded with humility, can lead to pride. We begin to think we achieved everything on our own, neglecting the God who provided and the people who helped us along the way.

Humility: The Key to Sustaining Blessings

Humility keeps us anchored when blessings come. James 4:6 (ESV) states, "God opposes the proud but gives grace to the humble." When we recognise that every good thing we have is a gift from God (James 1:17), we are more likely to remain thankful and compassionate.

Jesus himself modelled this. Though he was the Son of God, he humbled himself to serve others. Philippians 2:5-8 (NIV) tells us: "In your relationships with one another, have the same mindset as Christ Jesus: Who, being in very nature God, did not consider equality with God something to be used to his own advantage; rather, he made himself nothing by taking the very nature of a servant."

Blessings should never make us feel superior to others. Instead, they should remind us of our responsibility to lift others up.

Remembering Our Roots

One of the greatest failures of success is forgetting our past struggles. When Joseph became second in command in Egypt, he didn't use his position to build personal glory. Instead, he saved his family and an entire nation from famine (Genesis 41:39-57). He remembered where he came from and used his blessings to help others. He could be trusted with success.

Jesus himself said in Luke 12:48 (NIV): "From everyone who has been given much, much will be demanded; and from the one who has been entrusted with much, much more will be asked."

If God blesses us, it's not just for our own benefit. It's so that we can be a blessing to others.

Reaching Back to Help Others

Can we, in our success, reach back to help those still struggling? The Good Samaritan (Luke 10:25-37) didn't ignore the wounded man on the road. He used his resources to lift someone in need.

Success should expand our hearts, not harden them. True blessing is seen in how we use what we have to impact lives. Proverbs 11:25 (NIV) says, "A generous person will prosper; whoever refreshes others will be refreshed."

The Real Test of Blessing

The real test of blessing is not whether we receive it, but how we handle it. Do we let it make us arrogant, or do we use it to glorify God and uplift others? Do we remain humble and empathetic, remembering our own journey of struggles? If we cannot stand to be blessed with humility and generosity, then we risk losing the very thing we prayed for. So, can you stand to be blessed?

Theological Foundations of Godly Leadership

The biblical narrative consistently underscores the importance of humility in leadership. For example, Proverbs 11:2 (NIV) states, "When pride comes, then comes disgrace, but with humility comes wisdom." David exemplifies this wisdom throughout his reign. Despite his anointing and military victories, he remained acutely aware that his success was divinely ordained. In 1 Samuel 17, David attributes his victory over Goliath not to personal prowess but to the Lord's deliverance, reinforcing the principle that true leadership defers to God's sovereignty.

Similarly, Solomon's actions demonstrate wisdom and a deep commitment to justice. In 1 Kings 3:28, it is recorded that "when all Israel heard the verdict the king had given, they held the king in awe, because they saw that he had wisdom from God to administer justice." Solomon's leadership was not driven by personal ambition but by a divine calling to govern with discernment and equity. His famous judgment between the two women claiming to be the mother of the same child (1 Kings 3:16-27) exemplifies his ability to seek truth and ensure fairness.

Solomon's reign calls for a return to biblical wisdom, where authority is exercised for the flourishing of the community rather than self-promotion. Just as Solomon sought God's guidance (1 Kings 3:9), leaders today are encouraged to prioritize divine wisdom over personal gain. When leadership is rooted in justice and understanding, it becomes a source of blessing and stability for those under its care.

Challenges to Contemporary Leadership Models

This stands in stark contrast to many modern leadership models that equate power with control. Modern leadership often rewards visibility, influence, and personal ambition, fostering a culture of competition rather than service. This perspective challenges leaders to reconsider their motivations and methods. Jesus Himself rebukes the worldly understanding of leadership in Matthew 20:25-28, emphasising that "whoever wants to become great among you must be your servant." This radical redefinition of leadership calls for self-sacrificial service over self-promotion.

Furthermore, the biblical model challenges the transactional nature of contemporary success. Many leaders operate under the assumption that success grants entitlement rather than increased responsibility. David's example, and others however, demonstrate that success should lead to greater accountability before God and a commitment to ethical governance.

Encouragement for Today's Leaders

The call to biblical leadership is not an unattainable ideal but a divine invitation to reflect God's character in human endeavours. Adopting humility, stewardship, and generosity fosters personal integrity and strengthens communal well-being. Leaders in various spheres, whether in ministry, business, governance, families or academia, can cultivate environments and cultures where justice and faithfulness prevail. By doing so, they mirror the divine order and contribute to a leadership model that transcends mere success, embodying a legacy of godly influence.

Leaders who are secure within themselves do not need to be jealous, territorial, or unkind. They have nothing to prove. Instead, they can delegate responsibilities, regulate and genuinely celebrate the success of others without feeling threatened. Furthermore, they can honour the achievements of their predecessors and build upon the foundation they have laid. Such leaders foster a culture of trust, encouragement, and respect, not one of fear, intimidation, or low morale.

A fundamental measure of authentic leadership and moral greatness lies in how individuals treat those with less power or status, particularly those they are entrusted to serve. Leadership is not merely the exercise of authority, but the embodiment of ethical responsibility and empathy toward subordinates and constituents.

Managing success with humility and generosity remains a challenge, yet it is a hallmark of biblical leadership. David's example serves as both an inspiration and a standard, urging contemporary leaders to pursue a leadership ethic rooted in divine providence, fairness, and faithfulness. In embracing this call, leaders do not merely achieve success; they participate in God's redemptive work, shaping societies that honour Him through justice, humility, and service.

Chapter 8:
Reclaiming Your Lost Ground

— 99 —

Unwavering Faith

Fear and rejection are universal experiences that can paralyse even the strongest individuals, hindering them from stepping into their divine calling. However, overcoming them requires unwavering faith. The Bible is filled with examples of individuals who faced rejection and fear but triumphed through their trust in God.

Gideon, for instance, was overwhelmed with fear when God called him to lead Israel against the Midianites. He saw himself as the weakest in his family, yet God assured him, "I will be with you" (Judges 6:16, NIV). Despite his doubts, Gideon obeyed and witnessed God's power working through him.

Similarly, Moses hesitated at God's call, fearing he was inadequate for the task of leading Israel out of Egypt, but God equipped him to succeed. By understanding their stories and applying their faith principles, we can navigate challenges with confidence, knowing that God's plan prevails over human opposition. If fear has held you back, take heart, just as God strengthened Gideon and Moses, He will strengthen you.

Overcoming Fear and Rejection – A Journey of Faith

One of the most compelling biblical examples of faith in the face of rejection and fear is David. Before he became a great king, David was rejected and underestimated, even by those closest to him. When the prophet Samuel came to anoint Israel's next king, David's father, Jesse, did not even consider him worthy to be presented (1 Samuel 16:10-11). Yet, God had chosen David because of his heart, not his outward appearance (1 Samuel 16:7).

David's journey did not become easier after his anointing. King Saul, whom he faithfully served, turned against him, pursuing him with the intent to kill (1 Samuel 18:10-11). Yet, David did not allow fear or rejection to define him. Instead, he strengthened himself in the Lord (1 Samuel 30:6). His unwavering faith empowered him to face Goliath, declaring, "The battle is the Lord's" (1 Samuel 17:47, NKJV). David's trust in God not only led him to victory but also positioned him for the throne in due time.

Similarly, Gideon's story mentioned, reveals how God calls and equips those who feel inadequate. When the Lord called Gideon to deliver Israel, he hesitated, questioning his ability and background: "My clan is the weakest in Manasseh, and I am the least in my father's house" (Judges 6:15, NKJV). Yet, God reassured him, saying, "I will be with you" (Judges 6:16, NIV). Despite his doubts, Gideon obeyed and witnessed a miraculous victory with only 300 men, proving that God's power is made perfect in weakness (Judges 7:19-22, NIV).

Both David and Gideon illustrate that God does not require human strength or status to fulfil His plans. Their faith and obedience enabled them to overcome fear and adversity. Likewise, Esther displayed courageous faith when she risked her life to save her people, declaring, "If I perish, I perish" (Esther 4:16, NIV). Her trust in God led to divine favour and deliverance.

These accounts challenge us to trust God in the face of fear, rejection, or inadequacy. Like David, we must strengthen ourselves in the Lord. Like Gideon, we must step out in faith despite our doubts. Like Esther, we must stand boldly for God's purposes. The same God who called them is calling you today: will you trust Him?

Other Scriptural References on Overcoming Fear and Rejection

- Isaiah 41:10 (NIV) – "So do not fear, for I am with you; do not be dismayed, for I am your God. I will strengthen you and help you; I will uphold you with my righteous right hand."
- Psalm 27:10 (NIV) – "Though my father and mother forsake me, the Lord will receive me."
- Romans 8:31 (NIV) – "If God is for us, who can be against us?"
- 2 Timothy 1:7 (NKJV) – "For God has not given us a spirit of fear, but of power and of love and of a sound mind."

Here are some thought-provoking questions for you to contemplate:

1. How can you shift your perspective to see rejection as God's way of guiding you toward His perfect plan rather than a sign of failure?
2. Can you recall a time when rejection led you to something greater than you originally desired? How did that experience shape your faith?

3. What biblical figures experienced rejection but ultimately fulfilled God's purpose, and how can their stories inspire you to trust God's redirection?
4. How can you use moments of rejection to draw closer to God, seeking His wisdom and direction rather than dwelling on disappointment?

Faith as the Antidote to Fear and Rejection

Faith shifts the focus from human opposition to divine purpose. When we trust in God's promises, fear loses its grip. Consider the example of Daniel, who remained faithful to God despite the decree of King Darius that forbade prayer to anyone but the king.

Though Daniel was thrown into the lions' den as a result, he did not waver in his trust in God. Instead of being consumed by fear, he relied on God's power, and the Lord shut the mouths of the lions (Daniel 6:22). His story demonstrates that even in the face of persecution, God can use trials to reveal His glory and deliver His faithful ones.

In the New Testament, Jesus Himself faced rejection. Isaiah prophesied, "He was despised and rejected by mankind, a man of suffering, and familiar with pain" (Isaiah 53:3, NIV). Yet, He fulfilled His divine mission, demonstrating that rejection often precedes a greater calling.

Applying These Principles Today

In contemporary times, fear and rejection manifest in various ways: failed relationships, professional setbacks, financial reversals, societal exclusion, and personal insecurities. However, we can overcome by:

1. Anchoring Our Identity in Christ – Knowing that God's love is unwavering (Romans 8:38-39) enables us to stand firm.
2. Declaring God's Promises – Speaking scriptures over fears strengthens faith.
3. Viewing Rejection as Redirection – Trusting that God has a better plan than what was lost (Jeremiah 29:11).
4. Taking Bold Steps Despite Fear – Like Peter stepping out of the boat (Matthew 14:29), acting in faith leads to breakthroughs.
5. Encouraging Others – Supporting fellow believers fosters a community of faith and resilience (1 Thessalonians 5:11).

Fear and rejection are unavoidable parts of life, but they do not have to be permanent setbacks. By developing unwavering faith, we can turn these obstacles into stepping stones toward their divine purpose. Just as David, Joseph, and even Jesus overcame rejection through their trust in God, we can also walk in victory. The key lies in believing that rejection is often God's redirection and that faith in His promises will lead to ultimate fulfilment.

Navigating Moral Compromises with Integrity

Maintaining integrity can be challenging in a world where moral compromises are often justified for personal gain. Joseph, who refused to compromise his principles when tempted by Potiphar's wife (Genesis 39:7-12), is a model of unwavering character. He chose imprisonment over sin, demonstrating that integrity is not about convenience but steadfast commitment to God's principles (Proverbs 10:9).

In today's context, integrity in business, relationships, and personal conduct ensures long-term success and divine favour (Psalm 84:11). When faced with ethical dilemmas, standing firm in righteousness builds credibility and aligns us with God's higher plans (Matthew 6:33).

Challenge: Are there areas in your life where you are tempted to compromise? Ask God for the strength to remain steadfast, even when doing the right thing comes at a cost (James 1:12).

Encouragement: Remember, God honours those who walk in integrity. Just as He elevated Joseph in due time (Genesis 41:41-43), He will bless and uphold you when you choose righteousness over convenience (Galatians 6:9). Let us remain faithful, for our integrity is a testimony that glorifies God!

Adversity tests the strength of our faith, but it is in these moments that our dependence on God becomes essential. Think of Paul and Silas, imprisoned yet praising God, or Paul enduring shipwrecks and beatings. Nehemiah faced relentless opposition while rebuilding Jerusalem's walls, yet he pressed on with unwavering trust. David, when his city of Ziklag was burned and his people taken captive, could have given in to despair, but instead, he found strength in the Lord and sought His direction.

I want to encourage you: when you face loss, failure, or betrayal, do not let it break you. Instead, turn to prayer, scripture, and worship. Just as these men of faith overcame their trials, you too can cultivate spiritual resilience and position yourself for restoration and victory. God is with you, even in the most challenging moments. Stay strong and trust Him!

Strengthening Yourself in God When Faced with Adversity

Adversity often shakes the foundation of faith, but it is during these moments that reliance on God becomes crucial. David's experience in Ziklag, where he found his people captured and his city burned, illustrates this principle. Instead of succumbing to despair, he strengthened himself in the Lord and sought divine guidance. Today, individuals facing loss, failure, or betrayal can apply this lesson by immersing themselves in prayer, scripture, and worship. Doing so reinforces their spiritual resilience and positions them for restoration and victory.

Seeking Divine Guidance Before Making Critical Decisions

Making crucial decisions without seeking God's guidance can lead to disastrous consequences. Scripture repeatedly underscores the necessity of divine direction, as seen in Joshua's leadership when the Gibeonites deceived him because he "did not inquire of the Lord" (Joshua 9:14, NIV). This costly oversight serves as a sobering reminder that human wisdom alone is insufficient.

In today's world, decisions regarding career paths, relationships, finances, and other significant life choices must be made with God at the centre. Proverbs 3:5-6 (NIV), exhorts believers to "trust in the Lord with all your heart and lean not on your own understanding; in all your ways submit to Him, and He will make your paths straight."

When we make decisions without seeking God's guidance, it's easy to find ourselves praying for help when things go wrong. But the good news is that aligning our choices with God's perfect will can help us avoid unnecessary regrets and lead us to lasting peace and fulfilment. True, some decisions have lifelong consequences for which we must take responsibility. Nevertheless, no matter where we are, it's never too late to invite Him into the situation, even though we failed.

Through fervent prayer (Philippians 4:6-7), fasting (Matthew 6:16-18), and seeking wisdom from godly mentors (Proverbs 11:14), we can discern the right course. James 1:5 (NIV) reassures us, "If any of you lacks wisdom, you should ask God, who gives generously to all without finding fault, and it will be given to you." May we cultivate a habit of seeking God first in every decision, trusting that His wisdom far surpasses our own.

Recognising God's Plan Even in Setbacks

Setbacks often feel like failures, but are usually part of God's greater plan. Take Jesus, for example; His arrest, trial, and crucifixion seemed like a devastating defeat. His followers mourned, believing all hope was lost. Yet, what appeared to be the ultimate loss was the foundation for the most significant victory: His resurrection and the world's salvation.

When we face delays, disappointments, or unexpected hardships, we can remind ourselves that God is still at work, even when we do not understand. Sometimes what we perceive as a setback is simply life preparing us for a future beyond our comprehension.

If you feel like you have hit rock bottom, remember this: resurrection follows the cross. No matter how dark the night, morning always comes. "Weeping may endure for a night, but joy cometh in the morning" (Psalm 30:5, KJV). God specialises in bringing beauty from ashes (Isaiah 61:3), turning mourning into joy, and redeeming what was lost. Instead of letting despair define your story, believe God is still writing it. What feels like an ending may be the prologue to your greatest testimony. Hold on, trust Him, and watch how He turns your trials into triumphs.

Being Strategic in Choosing Battles

Not every conflict requires engagement. Exercising wisdom means discerning when to confront and when to remain silent. Jesus demonstrated this during His trial before the crucifixion, choosing not to argue with His accusers but entrusting Himself to God's plan (Matthew 26:62-63).

Similarly, David refrained from killing Saul, even when given the chance, recognising that vengeance belonged to God and that patience was key to fulfilling his destiny (1 Samuel 24:3-7). Another example is Solomon's handling of the two women disputing over a baby; rather than escalating the conflict, he used wisdom to reveal the true mother, resolving the issue peacefully (1 Kings 3:16-28).

Scripture also warns against engaging in pointless disputes: "But avoid foolish questions, and genealogies, and contentions, and strivings about the law; for they are unprofitable and vain" (Titus 3:9, KJV).

In modern life, choosing battles wisely involves knowing when to speak, when to let go, and when to stand firm. Strategic engagement helps prevent unnecessary strife and preserves energy for greater victories, whether in professional disputes, family conflicts, or social issues.

In Psalm 39:1 (KJV), we find these words: "I said, I will take heed to my ways, that I sin not with my tongue: I will keep my mouth with a bridle, while the wicked is before me." This verse reminds us of the power of our words and the importance of self-control, especially in the presence of those who seek to provoke or tempt us. David's commitment to guarding his speech teaches us that wisdom often lies in restraint.

In Proverbs 26:4-5 (KJV), we find these words: Answer not a fool according to his folly, lest thou also be like unto him. Answer a fool according to his folly, lest he be wise in his own conceit. Indeed, sometimes silence is wise, other times correction is necessary.

In Titus 3:9 (King James Version), the apostle as previously mentioned, advises: "But avoid foolish questions, and genealogies, and contentions, and strivings about the law; for they are unprofitable and vain." This verse underscores the importance of steering clear of pointless debates and divisive controversies, particularly those rooted in legalistic or speculative matters, as they contribute little to meaningful discourse and may hinder communal harmony.

When faced with difficult people or challenging situations, we can rely on God's guidance to help us respond with grace rather than react in anger. May this verse encourage you to seek patience and wisdom, knowing that a well-guarded tongue reflects a heart aligned with God's will. When you know who you are and whose you are, you have nothing to prove. Look at Jesus, we read in Isaiah 53:7 (KJV): "He was oppressed, and he was afflicted, yet he opened not his mouth: he is brought as a lamb to the slaughter, and as a sheep before her shearers is dumb, so he openeth not his mouth."

Understanding Both the Process and the Destination

In life, the pursuit of goals often overshadows the journey itself. Yet, the process of reaching a destination is where transformation truly occurs. We often become so fixated on achieving success, fulfilling dreams, or reaching milestones that we miss the lessons, growth, and refinement happening along the way. But God is not just concerned with where we are going. He is equally, if not more, concerned with who we are becoming in the process.

The story of the Israelites' journey to the Promised Land illustrates this truth powerfully. God was leading them to Canaan and shaping their hearts along the way (Deuteronomy 8:2-3). Their trials in the wilderness were not meaningless; rather, they were designed to refine their faith, teach dependence on God, and mould them into a people prepared to inherit His promises.

The delays, detours, and difficulties were not always punishments but rather divine preparation. However, it is also important to acknowledge that their unbelief and disobedience did lead to consequences, as seen in instances where they faced divine judgment, such as being denied entry into the Promised Land for a generation (Deuteronomy 8:2 and Numbers 14:32-33).

How often do we misinterpret our own seasons of waiting and hardship as obstacles rather than opportunities for growth?

Consider also Joseph's journey. He had a God-given dream of leadership, yet his path to fulfilment was anything but straightforward. Betrayed by his brothers, sold into slavery, falsely accused, and imprisoned, Joseph's character was tested at every turn. Yet, through it all, God was shaping him into the man who would one day rise to power and save many lives (Genesis 50:20). Had he arrived at his destiny too soon, he might not have been ready to handle it with wisdom, humility, and integrity. Are you willing to trust that God is using your challenges to prepare you for something greater?

Even Jesus Himself experienced this process. Before His public ministry, He spent 40 days in the wilderness, fasting and being tempted by Satan (Matthew 4:1-11). This time of testing was essential. It strengthened Him, solidified His dependence on the Father, and prepared Him for the mission ahead. If the Son of God had to go through a season of preparation, how much more should we expect the same? For if they do these things in the green tree, what shall be done in the dry? (Luke 23:31, KJV).

So, what about you? Are you resisting the process, frustrated by delays, or growing weary in the waiting? Or are you allowing God to shape you, refine you, and prepare you for what is ahead? The journey is not just a path to the promise; it is the place where God does His deepest work in you. Will you embrace it? Will you trust Him, even when the road is long and uncertain?

Let this be your challenge: Instead of merely enduring the process, engage with it. Ask God what He wants to teach you. Lean into the lessons, and allow Him to shape your heart. In the end, the transformation that happens along the way is often the greatest reward.

The Purpose in the Problem

It is easy to become discouraged when setbacks arise. However, Scripture reminds us that trials are not punishments but refining tools. James 1:2-4 (NIV), encourages believers to "consider it pure joy... whenever you face trials of many kinds, because you know that the testing of your faith produces perseverance." The refining process is difficult, yet necessary. Gold is purified in fire, and so are our lives through challenges (1 Peter 1:6-7). God cares deeply about who we become along the journey; that is our process, not just where we end up, our destination.

Hebrews 12:2 encourages us to keep our focus on Jesus, who is both the founder and fulfiller of our faith. He endured the cross, disregarding its shame, because of the joy set before Him, humanity's redemption, and His ultimate glory with God. His suffering was not meaningless, nor ours; just as He triumphed, we too can persevere through trials with hope. This verse reminds us that hardships are temporary, but God's promises are eternal. By fixing our eyes on Jesus, we find the strength to endure, knowing that the joy ahead far outweighs today's struggles.

Reclaiming Lost Ground

While the original passage with David, offers an inspiring message of divine restoration and forward momentum, it may benefit from a more nuanced acknowledgment of the complexity inherent in our personal and spiritual journeys. The assertion that "your story is not over" and that "the God who restores is also the God who propels you forward" reflects a theology of hope and resilience. However, the journey toward one's destiny is seldom linear. Setbacks and delays, whether circumstantial, emotional, or spiritual, often serve not merely as obstacles, but as formative experiences that shape both character and clarity of purpose.

To this end, it is important to recognize that detours are not necessarily denials; rather, they may signal a redirection or recalibration of one's path. The destination may evolve as understanding deepens, or the arrival may take longer than expected. Success, therefore, should not be narrowly defined by immediate outcomes but understood as a faithful progression toward divine purpose, even if the route changes.

Isaiah 40:31 (NIV) reminds us, "But those who hope in the Lord will renew their strength. They will soar on wings like eagles; they will run and not grow weary, they will walk and not be faint." Strength is found in persistence, and breakthrough comes through unwavering trust in God's promises. Do not settle for regret, move forward with courage, knowing that God's plans for you are still alive, waiting for your pursuit.

Hope for the Weary

If you find yourself in despair, know that your journey is not over. Every setback can be a setup for a comeback when God is in control (Romans 8:28). The road may be difficult, but you are not walking it alone. Isaiah 41:10 (NIV) reminds us, "Do not fear, for I am with you; do not be dismayed, for I am your God. I will strengthen you and help you; I will uphold you with my righteous right hand."

Trust that God is working even in the waiting, no matter where you are in your journey. Hold on. Keep believing. Your story is not finished, and the best is yet to come.

The Sovereignty of God in Life's Struggles

Life's challenges may have knocked you down, but they don't have the power to keep you there, unless you let them. As the wise saying goes: Failing is not falling down, but failing to get up! "For a just man falleth seven times, and riseth up again: but the wicked shall fall into mischief," Proverbs 24:16 (KJV).

This book is your call to rise, to fight, and to reclaim what is rightfully yours. *'Go Take It Back!'* is not just a book; it's a battle cry for those who refuse to let pain, loss, or failure define their future. You were made for more, and I challenge you to step into it.

You are not alone. You are not defeated. You are not forgotten.

Remember that as already mentioned, Joseph was betrayed by his brothers, thrown into a pit, sold into slavery, and unjustly imprisoned. Yet, he rose to lead a nation (Genesis 50:20). Jabez cried out to God for blessing and breakthrough, and God granted his request (1 Chronicles 4:10). Jacob wrestled with God and refused to let go until he received his blessing. His name and destiny were forever changed (Genesis 32:26-28). Paul was beaten, shipwrecked, and imprisoned, yet he declared, "I can do all things through Christ who strengthens me" (Philippians 4:13, NKJV). These stories are not just ancient history but proof that God still turns trials into triumphs.

And now it is your turn.

You may have faced rejection, loss, or overwhelming odds, but God is not finished with you. He is calling you to rise above the adversity, to see His hand at work even in the darkest moments, and to step boldly into the victory that is already yours. "The Lord upholds all who fall and lifts up all who are bowed down" (Psalm 145:14, NIV).

I fervently hope that through this book I will challenge you to see beyond your pain, encourage you to reclaim your joy, strengthen your faith, and empower you to take back what has been stolen. Your past does not define you. God does.

We are reminded in Proverbs 6:2 (KJV) that, "Thou art snared with the words of thy mouth, thou art taken with the words of thy mouth." This verse emphasises personal accountability, stating that we are trapped by our own words, not those of others. "If there is no enemy within, the enemy outside can do us no harm." (African Proverb).

This proverb emphasises the power of inner strength, self-discipline, and a clear conscience. It suggests that as long as we are at peace with ourselves in Christ, free from self-doubt, fear, or internal conflicts, external challenges or adversities will have little impact on us.

The Bible promises that "The Lord is close to the broken-hearted and saves those who are crushed in spirit." (Psalm 34:18, NIV). Now is the time to stand, fight, and take back your purpose, confidence, faith, and future.

Now is the time - go take it back!

My Rationale for This Book:

I intend to use this book to guide you through the journey of loss, faith, and restoration. I show that setbacks are not necessarily punishments but opportunities for growth. I highlight the power of faith in reclaiming what is lost, emphasising divine timing, humility, and generosity as keys to sustained blessings.

Healing from rejection and betrayal is undeniably challenging. However, we may find that restoration becomes possible when we take intentional and reflective steps toward renewal. We begin by rediscovering our sense of purpose, holding to the truth that our worth is not confined to past wounds (Jeremiah 29:11). Through prayer and thoughtful self-reflection, we can gain clarity about our identity and calling, gradually reclaiming the strength and direction that may have been obscured by pain.

Additionally, I also lean on the support of family, friends and a strong community because healing is not meant to be done alone. Surrounding myself with wise mentors and faith-filled friends helps me stay encouraged and accountable (Proverbs 27:17). Their support reminds me that God is near to the broken-hearted and will not forsake me (Psalm 34:18).

Even after experiencing restoration, I remain intentional about maintaining momentum by cultivating habits that reinforce my growth, through prayer, Scripture, and community (Romans 12:2). Healing is an ongoing process that requires trust in God's plan. I find encouragement in real-life testimonies of those who have been restored.

Their stories reinforce the transformative power of faith, reminding me that God works all things for good (Romans 8:28). No matter how deep the wounds of rejection, failure and even betrayal, His love brings healing, purpose, and hope to those who seek Him. Let us delve into this some more and highlight some key concepts:

Understanding Loss and Its Purpose: I understand that loss can be incredibly difficult to cope with, and it's completely natural to feel overwhelmed by setbacks. It's not easy to navigate these moments, and they can often feel overwhelming. But rather than seeing them as punishments, I try to embrace them as part of a larger journey, one that is shaping, refining, and preparing me for something greater.

Even though it is hard, I believe every challenge carries a deeper purpose, guiding me toward growth in ways I may not yet fully understand. In the midst of this struggle, I find myself echoing the words, "Lord, I believe; help Thou my unbelief" (Mark 9:24, KJV). Gaining closure in God's will is not always easy, and sometimes, surrendering to His plan feels like its own battle. But I hold on to the hope that, in time, His purpose will become clearer, even when the path is painful.

The Role of Faith in Restoration: I challenge you to stand firm in faith, even when the odds seem stacked against you. The stories in Scripture remind us that faith is the key to reclaiming what was lost and stepping into God's promises. Will you trust in His perfect timing and sovereignty, even when the path ahead looks impossible?

Take heart in the words of Philippians 4:13 (KJV): "I can do all things through Christ who strengthens me." Let this be your declaration, choosing faith over fear, resilience over doubt, and trust over despair. Your breakthrough is on the other side of unwavering belief. Will you rise to the challenge?

Embracing Divine Timing: Get ready to challenge your perspective on patience! Embrace the truth that restoration unfolds on God's divine timeline, not ours. Are you willing to trust Him even when waiting feels unbearable? Impatience can lead to frustration and poor decisions, but what if God's delays are actually strategic pauses designed to prepare you for something greater? Don't settle for doubt. Lean into faith, knowing that His timing is always perfect. Will you choose to wait with expectation, believing that His plan is worth it?

The Power of Humility and Generosity: Can you see success not as the finish line, but as a new beginning for even greater growth? True restoration and lasting blessings come not just from achievement, but from the humility to keep learning and the generosity to keep giving. A humble heart invites wisdom, and an open hand attracts abundance. Think about it; are you willing to use your success as a platform to uplift others? Can you embrace the power of humility and generosity to invite even greater favour into your life?

Practical Steps to Reclaim What Was Lost

To reclaim hope after despair, start by turning to prayer and thanksgiving; even in difficulty, just as Philippians 4:6-7 (NIV) says: "Do not be anxious about anything, but in every situation, by prayer and petition, with thanksgiving, present your requests to God. And the peace of God, which transcends all understanding, will guard your hearts and your minds in Christ Jesus."

"As a man thinketh in his heart, so is he" (Proverbs 23:7, NKJV). We are the products of our thoughts. The Bible also teaches in Romans 12:2 (NIV), "Do not conform to the pattern of this world, but be transformed by the renewing of your mind." Similarly, an African proverb earlier mentioned, states, "If there is no enemy within, the enemy without can do you no harm," reinforcing the power of inner strength. According to Les Brown, motivational speaker, 'Someone's (negative) opinion of me does not have to be my reality.'

To rebuild your mindset, take practical steps daily: Focus on small victories, whether through journaling, speaking positive affirmations, or setting achievable goals. Surround yourself with positivity: uplifting people, a healthy lifestyle, encouraging music, inspiring books, and reinforcing faith and resilience. You cultivate the strength to overcome external challenges by consistently nurturing yourself inwardly.

Engage in acts of service, as helping others shifts your perspective and brings joy, in line with Proverbs 11:25 (NIV): "A generous person will prosper; whoever refreshes others will be refreshed." Finally, prioritise self-care, get proper rest, exercise, and nourishment to strengthen both body and mind. These steps, along with faith, help rebuild hope and restore peace.

Rediscovering Purpose and Passion

When loss shakes your sense of purpose, it can feel like you're drifting without direction. But God has placed passions and callings deep within you, ones that no hardship can erase. Rediscover those gifts, realign with God's plan, and create a life of renewed meaning.

Through reflection, prayer, and intentional action, you will find that even in the midst of pain, God is still guiding you toward a future filled with hope. As Ephesians 2:10 (NIV) reminds us, "For we are God's handiwork, created in Christ Jesus to do good works, which God prepared in advance for us to do".

The Power of Association, Networking, and Accountability

Who you surround yourself with shapes your growth, success, and restoration. No one is an island; we thrive in community. Amos 3:3 reminds us that two cannot walk together unless they agree, while 1 Corinthians 15:33 warns that bad company corrupts good character. The correct associations challenge us, networking opens doors, and accountability keeps us on course. Faith communities, mentorship, and collective prayer strengthen and support our journey.

Forget not the assembling of yourselves together (Hebrews 10:25), for in unity, we find restoration, wisdom, and the push to become our best selves. Choose your circle wisely, for iron sharpens iron, and one man sharpens another (Proverbs 27:17, NIV).

Maintaining Momentum After Restoration: A Call to Persevere

Restoration is not the finish line. It is the starting point of a lifelong journey. Remain steadfast, guard against complacency, and continually pursue spiritual growth. Experience renewal is not enough; what you do after restoration defines your legacy.

King Hezekiah began well, leading with faith and devotion; however, his later years were marked by pride and short-sightedness (2 Kings 18–20; 2 Chronicles 29–32). His failure serves as a warning: even the strongest start can be undone without vigilance.

Let his story propel you to press on, using your renewed strength to uplift others and deepen your walk with God. True restoration isn't just about being revived, it's about sustaining the fire, finishing well, and leaving a legacy that honours God. Keep growing. Keep serving. Keep moving forward.

Testimonies of Reclaimed Lives: Life's journey often brings us to moments of loss, despair, and discouragement. In those moments, feeling abandoned, overwhelmed, or even hopeless is easy. Yet, you are not alone. Many have walked this path before you, including figures from the Bible; each facing their own trials and hardships. Their stories and real-life testimonies of today offer a beacon of hope, reminding us that through faith and perseverance, we can reclaim what has been lost and find joy again.

Reflecting on the insights from *Go Take It Back*! consider how you approach the challenges in your life. Are you seeing them as mere obstacles, or are you recognising them as divine opportunities for growth? What if every hardship was a moment for God to shape you, refine you, and draw you closer to His purpose? When you trust in His sovereignty, even pain gains meaning. Instead of resisting trials, lean in; ask, "What is God teaching me through this?"

Humility and generosity are not just virtues to admire but disciplines to practice. Are you actively making space in your life to serve others, to give freely, and to express gratitude? When you walk in humility, you open yourself to God's blessings, and when you live generously, you become a conduit of His love. True generosity isn't just about money; it's about your time, words, and kindness. So, how can you be more intentional today in embodying these values?

And don't walk this journey alone. Isolation is a tool of discouragement, but community is a source of strength. Are you plugged into a faith community that challenges, supports, and holds you accountable? Surround yourself with people who propel you toward God's best for your life. Find a place where you can grow, contribute, and be encouraged, because restoration flourishes in relationships.

So, take a step. Reflect. Act. What will you do today to reclaim what God has for you?

Chapter 9:
Go Take It Back: Strategies to Reclaim What You Have Lost – A Personal Reflection

— 🙶 —

Personal Reflection: Identifying My "Ziklag"

Life is an unpredictable journey, often filled with trials that test our faith, resilience, and endurance. There are moments when everything seems to be falling apart, dreams slipping away, relationships strained, opportunities lost, finances fading, health deteriorating and spiritual vitality fading. In these moments of despair, we may wonder where God is and whether restoration is possible.

Yet, Scripture reminds us that "The heart of man plans his way, but the Lord establishes his steps" (Proverbs 16:9, ESV). Though life may seem chaotic, God is sovereign over every detail. We are called to trust in Him rather than lean on our own understanding, for "In all your ways acknowledge Him, and He will make your paths straight" (Proverbs 3:6, ESV). Even when circumstances seem bleak, He is working all things together for good (Romans 8:28).

There may be times when everything you have built seems to be in ruins, returning to what should have been a place of security, only to find devastation. But here is the question: What will you do in that moment?

David sets us a great example. He didn't break under the weight of his suffering. When everything fell apart and even those closest to him turned against him, he did one thing, he turned to God. He cried. He grieved. But he didn't let grief consume him. He sought the Lord, and God gave him a command:

"Pursue, for you shall surely overtake them and without fail recover all" (1 Samuel 30:8).

And David obeyed. He fought back. He took back what was stolen.

So I ask you, who are you in this moment? Have you sought the Lord? Did you get a Word and if so, will you act upon it?

Are you like David's men, exhausted and bitter, struggling to hold on to faith? You've given everything, and yet you still face loss. But hear this: "The righteous cry out, and the Lord hears them; He delivers them from all their troubles" (Psalm 34:17, NIV). Even in exhaustion, God is faithful.

Or maybe you're like the two hundred exhausted, weary soldiers who had nothing left to give. You've been on the journey, but you're too weary to keep going. Yet your story doesn't end in failure. Jesus says, "Come to me, all you who are weary and burdened, and I will give you rest" (Matthew 11:28, NIV). Rest is not the end, it's preparation for what's next. Your gifts, talents and contribution are important.

There is however a permanent rest. "And I heard a voice from heaven saying, Write, Blessed are the dead which die in the Lord from henceforth: Yea, saith the Spirit, that they may rest from their labours; and their works do follow them." *Revelation 14:13 (KJV).*

Perhaps you feel like the abandoned Egyptian servant, left behind, forgotten, useless. But just as David's men found him, nourished him, and gave him a purpose, God has not forgotten you. "Do not fear, for I am with you; do not be dismayed, for I am your God. I will strengthen you and help you" (Isaiah 41:10).

Wherever you are in this story: worn out, broken, lost, know this, God meets you there. And He does not leave you in despair. But now comes the decision.

Will you let loss define you? Will you stay down, or will you rise? For 'Failing is not falling down, but failing to get up.'

"The righteous may fall seven times, but they rise again, while the wicked stumble when calamity strikes" (Proverbs 24:16, NIV).

This is your time. Your battle. Your restoration.

I know the temptation to give up. I know what it feels like to watch others move forward while you stay stuck. Despite their initial fears and doubts, David's men didn't let their brokenness keep them from the fight. And because they pressed on, with much encouragement of course, they were restored.

Now it is Your Turn.

God has spoken: **Pursue. Overtake. Recover all.**

So get up. Take back what was stolen. Walk in the victory God has already promised you.

The 200 Soldiers – Faithful, but Weary and Needing Rest

There are moments when even the most faithful grow weary, times when strength fails, and pressing forward feels impossible. The 200 soldiers in David's army who stayed behind were not weak in their devotion; they had simply reached their limit. Yet, David did not cast them aside or diminish their worth. Instead, he honoured them, ensuring they shared in the victory (1 Samuel 30:21-25). This challenges the belief that exhaustion equates to failure.

At times, we may lack the resilience and aspiration needed to push through difficulties, giving up too soon when faced with setbacks. Rather than viewing challenges as opportunities for growth, we may retreat, believing that success is out of reach. This mindset not only limits personal potential but also prevents the achievement of meaningful goals.

Resilience however, is not an inborn trait. It is developed through persistence, learning from failure, and believing in our ability to improve. If you feel like quitting, ask yourself: is this situation truly impossible, or have you just not found the right way yet? Push forward, because the greatest rewards often come to those who refuse to surrender.

How often does the pressure to keep striving lead to guilt over the need for rest? The world glorifies unrelenting effort, but God's ways are higher. He sees weariness not as a mark of inadequacy but as a call for renewal. "He gives strength to the weary and increases the power of the weak." (Psalm 29:11, NIV). The same God who led David's men to victory is the One who restores the exhausted and lifts those who stumble.

Jesus Himself demonstrated this truth. He did not demand ceaseless striving but invited the weary to come and receive rest: "Come to me, all you who labour and are heavy laden, and I will give you rest." (Matthew 11:28, ESV). More specifically, He encouraged his disciples saying to them, 'Come away by yourselves to a secluded place and rest a while. ' For there were many people coming and going, and they did not even have time to eat." Mark 6:31 (NASB).

Just as David refused to withhold the spoils of battle from those who needed to pause, Christ does not withhold His grace from those who must stop and be restored.

Psalm 23:3 (ESV) reminds us, "He restores my soul; He leads me in the paths of righteousness for His name's sake." God's renewal is not reserved for the strongest but is freely given to all who seek Him. Even Jesus, in His ministry, emphasized the necessity of abiding in Him rather than striving alone: "Abide in me, and I in you. As the branch cannot bear fruit of itself unless it abides in the vine, neither can you, unless you abide in me." (John 15:4, ESV). Strength is not found in unyielding effort but in staying connected to the true source of life.

Rest is not a retreat from purpose; it is part of God's design for endurance. Do not mistake exhaustion for exclusion from His blessings. He is the God who renews, restores, and rewards, even those who must pause along the way.

Elijah had just experienced a great spiritual victory on Mount Carmel, but afterwards, he fled in fear from Queen Jezebel. Exhausted and discouraged, he lay under a juniper tree, wanting to give up. That is when an angel appeared, provided food and water, and told him: "Arise and eat; because the journey is too great for thee." 1 Kings 19:7 (KJV)

The Abandoned Egyptian – Feeling Lost but on the Verge of Being Rescued

Feeling abandoned can be one of the most painful human experiences, leaving us questioning our worth and purpose. Like the Egyptian left to die, we may find ourselves in seasons of rejection and isolation, believing we have been discarded. But what if this abandonment is not the end of our story, but the turning point?

Just as David's kindness to the Egyptian led to a powerful redemptive moment, our moments of despair can be the very place where God orchestrates restoration. I cannot stress enough that what seems like rejection is often divine redirection, an opportunity for growth, renewal, and a transformative encounter with grace.

So, if you feel lost, forgotten, or struggling in silence: hold on. Your current pain is not your permanent reality. Just as the Egyptian was seen and rescued, you too are not invisible, and you are not without purpose.

Help is coming. Restoration is near. What was stolen: your hope, joy, or sense of belonging, can be reclaimed. Do not mistake this moment of hardship as the final chapter, because God is still writing your story, and rescue is already on its way. As the saying goes, 'Do not put a full stop where God puts a comma!' (Anon).

David: A Leader of Resilience, Vulnerability, and Decisive Action

The story of David reveals a leader who embodies both vulnerability and unwavering decisiveness in the face of adversity. Despite his strength, he does not shy away from fear or sorrow but embraces them as part of the human experience. When faced with loss, David does not react impulsively but instead allows himself and his men to grieve, acknowledging their pain before formulating a strategy to reclaim what was taken.

This approach to leadership has profound real-life applications. For example, often, in moments of crisis, we may suppress our emotions in favour of immediate action. However, David's example demonstrates that true strength lies in acknowledging fear and sorrow while maintaining the clarity to make strategic decisions. By accepting pain and vulnerability, we allow ourselves to fully process challenges, enabling us to act with wisdom rather than merely react. Scripture reminds us in Romans 12:15 (KJV) to "Rejoice with them that do rejoice, and weep with them that weep." Furthermore, give yourself permission to grieve in a healthy manner.

David's journey underscores an essential lesson: resilience is not about avoiding pain but about confronting it, processing it, and then taking decisive steps toward restoration. Whether in personal setbacks, professional challenges, or moments of collective loss, his example serves as a powerful reminder that embracing both vulnerability and action leads to true leadership and victory.

Similarly, Jehoshaphat, when faced with an overwhelming enemy, did not rely solely on human strength but turned first to God in humility and prayer. When Judah was under threat, he proclaimed a fast, gathered the people, and sought divine guidance (2 Chronicles 20:3-4). Instead of succumbing to fear, he acknowledged the reality of the danger and chose to place his trust in God's deliverance. The battle was not won by military might but by faith, worship, and obedience.

Like Jehoshaphat and David, you, too, may be standing in a moment of crisis. Pain, loss, and fear may cloud your vision, but you are not called to battle alone. Just as Jehoshaphat led his people to trust in God, and David found strength to recover what was lost, you too are called to hold on. Acknowledge your pain, but do not let it define you. Let it refine you. Turn to God, seek wisdom, and take the next step with courage.

Your greatest victories will not come from avoiding hardship but from facing it with faith, wisdom, and the determination to keep moving forward. Hold on, for restoration and victory come to those who refuse to surrender to despair.

Strengthen Yourself in the Lord

David did not let grief paralyse him. Instead, he "strengthened himself in the Lord" (1 Samuel 30:6). This is a powerful example for us today. Will we allow hardship to weaken our faith, or will we, like David, find strength in God?

Jesus also demonstrated this principle. He prayed in secret (Matthew 6:6), withdrew to be alone with the Father (Luke 5:16), and managed his relationships with intentionality. He fed the multitudes (Matthew 14:13-21), commissioned the seventy (Luke 10:1-17), and discipled the twelve (Mark 3:14). He also mentored three disciples: Peter, James, and John, allowing them to witness key moments, such as the Transfiguration (Matthew 17:1-9). Yet, in His most agonising hour in Gethsemane, He prayed alone (Luke 22:41-44). This is a powerful model for us to follow in relationship management.

If Jesus, the Son of God, needed solitude with the Father to endure suffering, how much more do we? Will we commit to strengthening ourselves in the Lord through prayer, worship, and His Word? Will we be intentional about our spiritual growth, seeking both solitude with God and wise fellowship? The choice is ours.

Take Decisive Action – Nehemiah's Example

Nehemiah saw the ruins of Jerusalem and didn't just mourn, he took action. But before he moved, he sought God's guidance through prayer and fasting (Nehemiah 1:4-11). When the time came, he boldly approached the king, gathered resources, and led the rebuilding effort.

What about you? Are there broken areas in your life: lost joy, purpose, vision, broken relationships or missed opportunities, that need restoration? Like Nehemiah, don't let fear, procrastination, severe opposition or hesitation hold you back. Seek God's wisdom, then step out in faith. The walls won't rebuild themselves. Will you rise and act?

Surround Yourself with the Right People

The people we surround ourselves with have a profound impact on our lives, shaping our mindset, resilience, and spiritual journey. In this story of David, his men, though initially fickle and discouraged, eventually stood by him and fought alongside him to reclaim what was lost (1 Samuel 30:6-8). Their unity and shared determination played a crucial role in their victory.

Similarly, I must be intentional about building relationships with those who uplift and strengthen me, people who will fight alongside me in times of struggle, encourage me when I feel defeated, and help me move forward in faith. Proverbs 27:17 (NIV) reminds us, "As iron sharpens iron, so one person sharpens another." Life's challenges can be overwhelming, but having the right people by my side can make all the difference, turning setbacks into stepping stones for growth.

Managing my associations and relationships is not just about avoiding negativity, but also about actively surrounding myself with those who inspire and challenge me to be better. The Bible warns against the influence of unhealthy relationships in 1 Corinthians 15:33 (NIV): "Do not be misled: 'Bad company corrupts good character.'" The right people will push me toward my goals, keep me accountable in my faith, grounded in success and remind me of my purpose if I appear to be losing sight of it.

Just as David's men supported him despite their initial doubt, I should seek friendships and connections that stand firm in both trials and triumphs. Friends who can respect the principle of reciprocity. Ecclesiastes 4:9-10 (NIV) emphasises the value of strong relationships: "Two are better than one… If either of them falls, one can help the other up."

A strong support system fosters perseverance and fuels my ability to reclaim what may seem lost, helping me walk confidently in the direction God has called me. Therefore, I must be discerning, prioritizing relationships that align with my values and propel me toward a life of faith, growth, and purpose.

Recognise that Your Pain Serves a Greater Purpose

Have you ever considered that your pain isn't pointless? That your struggles, though deeply personal, might actually be a crucial part of someone else's breakthrough? Just as the abandoned Egyptian in 1 Samuel 30:11-15 held the key to David's victory, your own hardships may be the bridge to someone else's restoration. No suffering is wasted in God's hands. He redeems and restores for His greater glory.

Think about Ruth. She lost everything: her husband, her home and her security. Yet, in the midst of her grief, she chose faith over fear, saying to Naomi, "Where you go I will go, and where you stay I will stay. Your people will be my people and your God my God" (Ruth 1:16, NIV). Her pain set her on a path that led not just to personal redemption but to a place in the lineage of Jesus Christ.

So, what about you? Will you allow your pain to push you closer to purpose? Will you trust that God is using every tear, fear, care or every trial, for something beyond what you can see? Stand firm, your story isn't over. Your suffering will serve a purpose greater than you ever imagined.

Through faith, perseverance, and divine guidance, I will recover what was stolen. God meets me where I am and restores what was lost. The time for mourning is over. God tells Joshua to stop mourning Moses' death and arise to lead the Israelites into the

Promised Land (Joshua 1:2). I have had my period of grieving. It is time to rise, pursue, and reclaim my destiny. Now is the time. Go, take it back!

Embracing Restoration with Faith and Action

This is your call to action. *Go Take It Back* is your guide to reclaiming what was lost: your hope, your voice, your purpose. You will walk through the real terrain of rejection, loss, and adversity, not to be defeated by them, but to uncover the path to restoration. Understand this: your setbacks are not dead ends. They are divine detours; preparation for the victories ahead. Now is the time to rise, to reclaim, and to move forward with faith and bold action.

Analysis of Key Themes

Throughout the book, I highlight and address several recurring themes that emerge:

- **Unwavering Faith in the Face of Adversity:** Like David confronting Goliath or Joseph standing firm against moral compromise, the narrative reminds us that faith is the cornerstone of overcoming life's most daunting challenges. The trials we encounter are not mere obstacles but opportunities for spiritual growth and resilience.

- **Divine Redirection Amid Rejection:** When rejection and betrayal appear insurmountable, they often serve as precursors to greater blessings. As illustrated by the biblical accounts, what initially seems like a loss can be a redirection toward a higher destiny.

- **Integrity and Strategic Engagement:** In a world rife with moral compromises, maintaining integrity becomes a testament to one's character. In this book, I evaluate the wisdom of choosing battles carefully and demonstrate that sometimes, restraint and discernment are the very actions that pave the way for restoration.

- **The Transformative Journey:** Emphasising that the process is as crucial as the destination, the narrative shows that our personal transformation is forged in the crucible of trials. The journey itself, marked by perseverance, prayer, community support, personal resilience, and decisive action, is what truly refines us. Furthermore, success must be carefully managed to remain humble, empathetic, and grounded.

Evaluation of the Strategies

The strategies I have outlined in this book are both timeless and highly relevant to contemporary challenges. I emphasise the importance of strengthening ourselves in God, noting that personal renewal begins with spiritual fortification. Immersing ourselves in prayer, scripture, and worship serves as a foundation for inner strength and resilience.

I also highlight the necessity of **seeking divine guidance**, so that we can prioritise discernment and wisdom over impulsive decisions. By aligning both heart and mind with God's will, we can navigate life's critical choices with greater clarity and purpose.

Understanding that restoration is not a solitary endeavour, I underscore the value of **community and accountability**. Surrounding ourselves with supportive and uplifting relationships that foster growth and provide necessary guidance along the journey. However, at times, people will inevitably fail and disappoint us. We need to balance criticism with compliments and stand resolute, knowing and accepting our identity in Christ.

I also emphasised the importance of **decisive action coupled with humility**, striking a balance between boldness and a humble spirit. The restoration that we achieve is not merely for personal benefit but also as a means to bless and inspire others.

Application: Reclaiming Your Lost Ground Today

The insights I present in this book offer some suggestions and principles for personal transformation and restoration. Consider the following practical steps to reclaim what has been lost and reclaim hope after despair:

- **Embrace a Divine Perspective on Trials:** View setbacks as part of a larger, divinely orchestrated plan. Reflect on how your current challenges might be preparing you for greater victories.

- **Cultivate Unwavering Faith:** Regularly engage in prayer, meditation, and the study of scripture to fortify your inner strength. Let your faith be the foundation upon which you rebuild your life.

- **Seek Wise Counsel and Community:** Surround yourself with a community that shares your values. Engage in honest conversations and seek mentorship from those who have navigated similar challenges.

- **Act with Integrity and Deliberation:** Make decisions that honour your values. When faced with ethical dilemmas, remember that true restoration comes from steadfast adherence to divine principles, even if it means temporary setbacks.

- **Recognise and Transform Pain:** Understand that your personal struggles have a purpose. Use your experiences to help others, transforming your pain into a testimony of hope and resilience.

Embrace Your Remaining Strengths and Shift Your Focus

No matter how deep the sorrow, hope is never lost. Revelation 21:4 (NIV) reminds us, "He will wipe every tear from their eyes. There will be no more death or mourning or crying or pain, for the old order of things has passed away." Though loss may weigh heavy on your heart, God calls you to embrace the strength that remains within you. Shift your focus from what has been taken to what still stands firm: your faith, resilience, and the boundless love of God.

Revelation 3:8 (NIV) declares, "See, I have placed before you an open door that no one can shut." Even in despair, there is an open door ahead, a new path filled with grace and opportunity. Step forward with courage, knowing that your future is still held in divine hands. Walk through you open door!

Gradual Healing and Rebuilding

Healing is a journey: a process that unfolds step by step, requiring both acknowledgement of past wounds and the determination to move forward. The biblical story of Jacob vividly illustrates this process. Initially known as a trickster and a supplanter, Jacob deceived his brother Esau and schemed to obtain both the birthright and the blessing (Genesis 25:29–34; 27:1–40, NIV). Yet, his life was not solely defined by deception; it became a journey of transformation and divine encounter.

He underwent a profound transformation through struggle and divine encounters. His wrestling with the angel at Peniel (Genesis 32:22-32) symbolises the painful but necessary confrontation with our own flaws and hardships. Just as Jacob had to face his past, healing begins with honest recognition of pain. It is only by naming and understanding our struggles that true progress can be made. As the saying goes, 'step one in problem-solving is recognition of the problem.' (Anon).

Yet, acknowledgment alone is not enough; healing also requires intentional steps toward renewal. After his struggle, Jacob received a new name, 'Israel', signifying a shift in identity and purpose. This mirrors the process of healing for us, where small, consistent actions; setting attainable goals, building healthy habits, and celebrating progress, lead to meaningful change.

Just as Jacob's journey was marked by prolonged trials, personal failures, and eventual reconciliation with his brother Esau, the process of healing, whether emotional, physical, or spiritual is seldom immediate. Rather, it unfolds gradually, shaped by perseverance, faith, and the accumulation of small victories. Jacob, once known as a deceiver and manipulator, underwent a deep transformation and was ultimately renamed *Israel*, a name meaning "he struggles with God" (Genesis 32:28, NIV) and became the father of a great nation.

However, this transformation did not come without cost. After wrestling with God, Jacob was left with a permanent limp, a physical reminder of his struggle (Genesis 32:31, NIV). This limp serves as a powerful metaphor: one can be blessed, even chosen, and still carry the marks of past pain. Success and spiritual growth do not erase hardship, but rather weave it into a greater story of redemption.

The limp challenges overly idealistic views of victory by reminding us that real transformation often includes visible or invisible signs of struggle. In this way, Jacob's blessing was not about removing his weakness but giving it deeper meaning; a sign that wounds and strength can co-exist.

Reclaiming Your Power - Identifying What Remains

Elijah stood on Mount Carmel, witnessing the fire of God consume the sacrifice before the worshippers of Baal (1 Kings 18:38, ESV). But just days later, he found himself fleeing into the wilderness, convinced that all was lost (1 Kings 19:3-4, ESV). Fear and exhaustion clouded his vision, making him forget the power he had just witnessed.

Jezebel's threats paralyzed Elijah with fear, causing him to focus on his impending doom rather than the victories God had already given him (1 Kings 19:2, ESV). He saw only danger and despair, but God saw a future, one where Elijah would anoint kings and call forth new leaders (1 Kings 19:15-17, ESV).

Yet, even in his despair, God met him, not in the wind, nor the earthquake, but in a still small voice, reminding him of what remained (1 Kings 19:11-12, ESV).

Scripture reminds us: "Yet I reserve seven thousand in Israel, all whose knees have not bowed down to Baal and whose mouths have not kissed him." (1 Kings 19:18, NIV). Although Elijah felt isolated and exhausted, he was not truly alone, for God had preserved a faithful remnant.

So too, when loss threatens to consume us, we must take stock of what still endures. Identify the resources, skills, relationships, and inner strengths that have not been taken from you. Like Elijah, who still had his prophetic calling despite his fear (1 Kings 19:15-16, ESV), you too have resources left untouched. Recognising what remains is the first step in reclaiming what feels lost.

Focusing on Possibility Over Loss

Rather than fixating on what has been stripped away, shift your gaze to what can be built anew. Loss, though deeply painful, is not the conclusion of your journey. Rather than focusing on what is missing, see this moment as an opportunity for renewal and transformation.

Trust that even in hardship, there is purpose ahead. "The Lord is near to the broken-hearted and saves the crushed in spirit." (Psalm 34:18, NIV).

Identify the strengths that remain and develop a plan based on them. In doing so, the narrative shifts from one of loss to a demonstration of resilience.

Step-by-Step Rebuilding

God did not restore Elijah's strength in an instant. He first sent an angel to provide food and rest (1 Kings 19:5-7), then led him to Mount Horeb for a deeper revelation (1 Kings 19:8-9). Healing and restoration are not immediate; they are step-by-step processes that require patience and perseverance in grief.

Embrace this gradual rebuilding. "Do not despise these small beginnings, for the Lord rejoices to see the work begin" (Zechariah 4:10, ESV). Set small, achievable goals and celebrate each step forward. Whether it's reclaiming confidence, restoring relationships, or pursuing long-buried dreams. Acknowledge every victory, no matter how small. Just as Elijah's journey required nourishment and divine guidance before he could walk in renewed purpose, your path to restoration could unfold one step at a time.

Transforming Loss into Opportunity

Elijah's lowest point became the catalyst for a new chapter. God gave him a renewed mission; anointing Elisha, Jehu, and Hazael (1 Kings 19:15-16, ESV). What seemed like the end was actually the beginning of something much greater.

Your loss, however painful, creates space for transformation. Instead of seeing setbacks as dead ends, view them as divinely orchestrated redirections. Let us consider the verse, "The Lord our Rehoboth has made room for us, and we shall be fruitful in the land" (Genesis 26:22, NKJV). What may seem like an ending is often the beginning of something greater, an opportunity for growth and renewal.

Therefore, "Lengthen your cords and strengthen your stakes" (Isaiah 54:2, NIV), for God is making space for His purpose to unfold in your life and increase the sphere of your influence. Trust that He is leading you into a season of abundance and new beginnings. Each challenge can be a stepping stone toward a stronger, wiser version of yourself. By trusting that God is at work even in difficulty, you reclaim not only what was lost but also what is yet to be gained.

The journey of "taking back" what was lost is not about dwelling on what has slipped away but about rediscovering what remains and using it to build something new. "Behold, I am doing a new thing; now it springs forth, do you not perceive it?" (Isaiah 43:19, ESV).

Just as Elijah emerged from his despair with a renewed sense of purpose, you too can rise from loss with a fresh vision. Actively reclaim your power, focus on possibilities, rebuild patiently, and allow loss to transform into opportunity. In doing so, you will not only heal but also craft a future rooted in resilience, faith, and God's unshakable promises.

Chapter 10:
Final Challenge: Reclaim What You Have Lost – Hope After Despair

— 99 —

Understanding Despair and Hope

Hope is not merely a fleeting emotion. It is a powerful anchor for the soul. As the Bible reminds us, "We have this hope as an anchor for the soul, firm and secure" (Hebrews 6:19, NIV). Yet for many who have endured prolonged despair, whether through trauma, failure, or deep heartache, hope can seem unreachable. In its place, a quiet numbness or persistent fear settles in.

The journey back to hope is rarely straightforward. It is often blocked by emotional wounds, distorted beliefs, and the scars of experiences that taught us not to trust in others, in ourselves, or even in God.

In this chapter I would like to explore some barriers to reclaiming hope and confidence. This include the deep erosion of self-belief, the effects of childhood trauma, and the complexities of our nature and nurture. In the face of despair, we are invited to rest in God's presence and truth, even when we cannot yet see the way ahead.

Barriers to Reclaiming Hope

If you've ever felt like hope is slipping through your fingers, you're not alone. One of the greatest barriers to reclaiming hope is the slow erosion of confidence. In this section, we will look at how life's wounds; like rejection, disappointment, or abandonment, can make us doubt your ability to move forward. But take heart: God has not left us powerless. Let's rediscover together the strength and assurance He has already placed within us.

The Erosion of Confidence

When despair takes root, confidence often withers. It becomes hard to believe that anything we do matters, or that we are capable of change. This erosion happens slowly, through painful experiences, for instance, rejection, abandonment or disappointment. Over time, we start to feel as though we are spectators in our own lives, powerless to act or hope.

But Scripture reminds us of our God-given agency: "For God gave us a spirit not of fear but of power and love and self-control" (2 Timothy 1:7, ESV). Even when confidence fades, the Spirit within us is not shaken. The challenge lies in reconnecting with that truth when despair has distorted our inner vision.

Nature and Nurture

The long-standing debate between nature and nurture offers some insight into why certain individuals struggle more deeply with despair. On one hand, biology does play a role. Some are naturally more sensitive to anxiety due to their genetic makeup. As Psalm 139:14 (NIV) reminds us, "I praise you because I am fearfully and wonderfully made; your works are wonderful, I know that full well." Each person is uniquely designed by God, including their emotional wiring.

On the other hand, our environment also profoundly shapes us. A nurturing upbringing filled with love, affirmation, and faith can provide a strong foundation for resilience. Conversely, an environment marked by fear, neglect, or instability can deepen emotional wounds and make hope harder to grasp. Proverbs 22:6 (ESV) encourages, "Train up a child in the way he should go; even when he is old he will not depart from it." This highlights the formative power of nurture.

However, it's important to approach this topic with both compassion and nuance. While a loving home can offer great advantages, it does not guarantee emotional health or spiritual flourishing. Similarly, a painful or neglectful upbringing does not seal someone's fate. Scripture is full of individuals who rose above painful pasts: Joseph, Moses, and even Jesus, who "was despised and rejected by men" (Isaiah 53:3, ESV), yet fulfilled a redemptive purpose.

Ultimately, both nature and nurture matter, but neither fully defines a person. God's grace transcends both, offering healing, transformation, and hope beyond what biology or background might predict. As 2 Corinthians 5:17 (NIV) assures us, "If anyone is in Christ, the new creation has come: The old has gone, the new is here!"

The Bible acknowledges the impact of our upbringing but also speaks to the transformative power of God in our lives: "Though my father and mother forsake me, the Lord will receive me" (Psalm 27:10,NIV). Even when our nurturing was inadequate, God Himself steps in to 're-parent' and restore what was lost.

Childhood Trauma and the Disruption of Hope

Trauma in childhood, whether it be neglect, abuse, or instability, deeply impacts the developing nervous system. The child becomes hyper vigilant or shuts down emotionally. In adulthood, this can manifest as chronic anxiety, numbness, or being stuck in patterns of avoidance.

These responses are not signs of weakness; they are survival strategies. However, when trauma defines our default state, hope becomes foreign. It's hard to trust in God's goodness or in a hopeful future when your body is constantly preparing for threat.

And yet, Scripture offers a healing invitation: "Come to me, all you who are weary and burdened, and I will give you rest" (Matthew 11:28, NIV). In Christ, there is rest for our bodies and peace for our overwhelmed hearts.

Internalised Narratives

One of trauma's most cruel legacies is the false narrative it implants. For example, "I am unworthy," "Nothing will ever change," "I am too broken." These beliefs take root in silence and shame. As adults, we may not even realise how often we agree with these lies.

But the Word of God cuts through every false voice: "I will praise thee; for I am fearfully and wonderfully made: marvellous are thy works; and that my soul knoweth right well." *Psalm 139:14* (KJV). "You are altogether beautiful, my darling; there is no flaw in you" (Song of Solomon 4:7, NIV). "For we are God's masterpiece…" (Ephesians 2:10, NLT). Healing involves not just therapy or reflection, but also replacing lies with the truth of who God says we are. Your identity is in Christ. "For he hath made him to be sin for us, who knew no sin; that we might be made the righteousness of God in him." 2 Corinthians 5:21 (KJV)

Why It Is So Hard to Be Confident Again

Confidence isn't simply about self-esteem. It is rooted in knowing who you are and whose you are. When we've been wounded, especially in formative years, confidence doesn't come back quickly. It must be rebuilt, often from the ground up. The world's message is to perform, to prove, to strive. But God calls us to rest in Him and to "be strong and courageous… for the Lord your God goes with you; he will never leave you nor forsake you" (Deuteronomy 31:6, NIV).

True confidence begins with surrender, laying down our fear and allowing the Holy Spirit to remind us of our identity as beloved children of God. From this place, courage can rise again. But we must also remember that faith without works is dead; like David at Ziklag, we are called not only to believe but to rise, strengthen ourselves in the Lord, and take bold, Spirit-led action.

Encouragement and Empowerment: A Path Forward

Though the journey from despair to hope may be long, we are never alone. God walks with us, even in the valleys. Healing is real. Restoration is possible. And the promise of Scripture is that what was lost can be redeemed. One of our key verses remain: "I will restore to you the years that the locusts have eaten…" (Joel 2:25, ESV).

Steps to Healing and Recovery

Healing is a journey, not a destination. It takes time, grace, and intentional steps rooted in faith. This section offers practical ways to walk with God through your healing process. Each step is designed to help you reconnect with Him, process your pain, and find renewed strength and peace. As you move forward, remember: it's not about doing everything perfectly. It's about surrendering your brokenness to the One who restores.

Here are key steps to guide your healing and recovery:

1. Daily Time in the Word and Prayer

- Set aside a consistent time each day; morning, evening, or whenever you're most focused to read Scripture and talk with God.

- Why it Heals: It aligns your heart with God's truth, calms anxiety, and builds trust in His presence and promises.
- Scripture Focus: "Your word is a lamp to my feet and a light to my path" (Psalm 119:105, ESV).

2. Honest Confession and Heartfelt Surrender

- Journaling your pain, confessing your struggles in prayer, and releasing control over situations to God.
- Why it Heals: It removes spiritual burdens and creates space for God's peace to enter in.
- Scripture Focus: "Cast all your anxiety on him because he cares for you" (1 Peter 5:7, NIV).

3. Connecting with a Faith-Filled Community

- Join a small group, attend a Bible study, or simply share life with trusted believers.
- Why it Heals: Others can remind you of truth when you're weary, pray for you, and reflect God's love.
- Accountability in community often leads to lasting transformation.
- Scripture Focus: "And let us consider how we may spur one another on toward love and good deeds, not giving up meeting together, as some are in the habit of doing, but encouraging one another, and all the more as you see the Day approaching." (Hebrews 10:24–25, NIV).

4. Embracing Rest and Stillness

- How to Practice: Take intentional time away from noise; no phone, no TV, just sitting in God's presence, possibly with soft worship music or in silence.
- Why it Heals: Stillness allows you to reconnect with God and yourself without distraction.

- Scripture Focus: "Be still, and know that I am God" (Psalm 46:10, NIV).

Healing is not about striving to be perfect; it's about trusting that God is making something beautiful out of brokenness.

Empowered to Recover

In every season of loss, God extends a divine invitation to rise again; not in your own strength, but through His. Recovery is not merely about regaining what was taken; it's about stepping into a deeper awareness of your God-given identity and purpose. Spiritually, emotionally, and even physically, you are being shaped and prepared for restoration that exceeds what you once imagined. The process may be painful, but the promise is powerful: through Christ, you are not only capable of enduring—you are empowered to overcome.

"But those who hope in the Lord will renew their strength. They will soar on wings like eagles; they will run and not grow weary, they will walk and not be faint." (Isaiah 40:31, NIV)

This is your moment to rise. This is your moment to shine! Every setback, whether it's lost time, dwindled faith, disrupted careers, broken relationships, or missed opportunities, has prepared you for this pivotal challenge and moment in time. With resilience, determination, and grit, alongside unwavering prayer and faith in God, you are empowered to recover everything that was once lost. This is not just about reclaiming the tangible. It's about restoring your spirit and reigniting the fire within you. Recognise that there is greatness within you. That fire that burns so brightly to illuminate the path to purpose and destiny. That nagging lingering thought that, 'I can do and be more than this! "I can do all things through Christ who strengthens me." (Philippians 4:13, NKJV)

Life Application: Steps to Take Back Your Life

This section is designed to help you move from inspiration to implementation. Healing, restoration, and personal growth don't happen by accident. They require intention, discipline, and faith. Here, we reflect on the key principles you've encountered so far, and offer you tangible ways to apply them in your daily life.

Each point includes a challenge task; a practical step for you to contemplate and complete, designed to anchor spiritual truth in everyday action. These are not meant to overwhelm, but to help you move forward with courage, faith, and clarity.

James 1:22 (NIV) reminds us, "Do not merely listen to the word, and so deceive yourselves. Do what it says." Now is the time to take the truths you've received and walk them out in faith.

These points are worth reiterating. Carve out moments of quiet reflection. In a world filled with noise and distractions, intentional stillness allows you to hear God's voice more clearly. Isaiah 30:15 (KJV) reminds us that '…In returning and rest shall ye be saved; in quietness and in confidence shall be your strength…'

Turn to God in prayer, seeking His guidance for strength, wisdom, and clarity. Recognise that every loss holds a lesson, and every challenge paves the way for a fresh start.

As you reflect, consider the words of Mark 11:24 (NLT): "I tell you, you can pray for anything, and if you believe that you've received it, it will be yours." Prayer aligns your heart with God's purpose, preparing you for the restoration ahead.

Challenge: Will you commit to a daily practice of seeking God's wisdom before making decisions? Start today by setting aside time for focused prayer and reflection.

Embrace Resilience and Determination

Understand that the journey to recovery is gradual. Healing and restoration do not happen overnight. Commit to daily actions; no matter how small, that steer you toward your goals. Whether it's reclaiming your time, rebuilding your career, or mending relationships, each step forward is a victory.

Remember Joshua 1:9 (NLT): "This is my command, be strong and courageous! Do not be afraid or discouraged. For the Lord your God is with you wherever you go." Strength does not come from your own efforts alone but from the power of God working within you. "The eternal God is your refuge, and underneath are the everlasting arms. He will drive out your enemies before you, saying, 'Destroy them!'" Deuteronomy 33:27, NIV).

Challenge: What small but meaningful action will you take today to step closer to your goal? Identify one area where you can exercise resilience and take that first step.

Harness the Power of Perseverance

Challenges are inevitable. At times, the road to reclaiming your life may seem overwhelming, but grit, passion and perseverance will keep you moving forward. When obstacles arise, remind yourself of the strength that lies within. Romans 5:3-4 (NLT) teaches us: "We can rejoice, too, when we run into problems and trials, for we know that they help us develop endurance. And endurance develops strength of character, and character strengthens our confident hope of salvation." With unwavering faith, you can overcome hurdles that once seemed insurmountable.

Challenge: When faced with difficulties, will you push forward with faith or retreat in fear? Make a choice today to persist, even in the face of adversity.

Trust in God's Promises

Anchor your journey in faith. God's promises are a foundation that will never crumble. He assures you that restoration is possible, that He is working all things for your good. Meditate on Isaiah 41:10 (NLT): "Don't be afraid, for I am with you. Don't be discouraged, for I am your God. I will strengthen you and help you. I will hold you up with my victorious right hand." Let His promises remind you that your best days are ahead.

Challenge: Will you trust God fully, even when the future is uncertain? Take time today to write down and then memorise at least one promise from Scripture that speaks to your current struggles.

Develop a Practical Action Plan

Faith without action is incomplete. Take intentional steps toward reclaiming every area of your life. Outline clear, achievable goals in your personal, professional, and spiritual life. Whether it is planning career moves, nurturing relationships, or launching a new venture, be specific about your next steps.

Seek wise counsel from mentors and prayer partners who share your vision of recovery. Proverbs 16:3 (NLT) advises: "Commit your actions to the Lord, and your plans will succeed." Your action plan should align with God's purpose for your life, ensuring that every step leads to lasting fulfilment.

Challenge: Will you create a written plan for your personal growth and accountability? Start by listing three goals and the steps needed to achieve them. These should be Specific, Measurable, Achievable, Realistic and Time-bound (SMART).

Your Call to Action

Today, choose to take back what is rightfully yours. The lost time, the faltering faith, the disrupted dreams, all can be restored with persistent effort and divine support. Stand firm in the knowledge that your resilience, combined with God's grace, will transform every trial into triumph. Ephesians 4:23-24 (NLT) encourages us: "Instead, let the Spirit renew your thoughts and attitudes. Put on your new nature, created to be like God, truly righteous and holy." This is your moment to reclaim your life.

Challenge: Will you take action today? Let this be the day you draw a line in the sand and commit to a renewed life, where every day is an opportunity to rebuild, reclaim, and rejoice in the abundance of what is yet to come.

Chapter 11:
Reclaiming What I Personally Lost and Choosing Hope After Despair

—————— 99 ——————

As I stand at this juncture of my life, reflecting on the journey that has brought me here, I am reminded of that special afternoon at school when a simple act of kindness altered my path significantly. The weight of responsibility, particularly at home, had worn me down, and I was not really aware of it. Yet it was the compassion of one teacher, Mrs. Dunkley that illuminated the power of empathy, care, and support through her timely intervention.

Her willingness to listen, to see beyond my role as Head Boy and into the heart of a student struggling under the weight of my domestic chores, reminds me of Proverbs 11:25 (NIV): "A generous person will prosper; whoever refreshes others will be refreshed." She not only saw my struggles but guided me toward rest and renewal, just as Christ calls us in Matthew 11:28 (NIV), "Come to me, all who are weary and burdened, and I will give you rest."

That moment was not just an encouragement to seek help but an awakening; a call to live a life defined by awareness of my humanity, rest, relaxation and balance. My mother's selflessness in prioritising my well-being over the financial necessity of our home affirmed this lesson, reflecting the spirit of Philippians 2:4

(ESV), "Let each of you look not only to his own interests but also to the interests of others."

The sacrifices she and my late father made reinforced my belief that true strength is found not in relentless toil but in the courage to care, to nurture, and to uplift. Not only to work hard, but also to work smart.

This lesson shaped my career and my calling. Choosing to enter the field of education was not simply a professional decision, it was a mission and vocation now spanning at the time of this publication (2025), over 43 years. Inspired by those who had uplifted me, I sought to create learning environments where students would not just gain knowledge, but where they would be seen, heard, loved, inspired, encouraged, empowered and challenged.

Like the Good Samaritan in Luke 10:33-34, I endeavour to extend care to those in need, ensuring that no student under my charge feels unseen or unheard. I have come to understand that education is not solely about intellectual development but about shaping character, inspiring hope, and preparing young minds for a future of purpose and integrity. I want to be an encourager, someone that they can turn to for reassurance, nurture, and safety in a non-judgmental way.

My academic aims include developing self-confidence and a sense of responsibility, enabling informed life choices, fostering positive relationships, respecting differences, and preparing pupils for the experiences, opportunities, and responsibilities of adult life.

The Power of Words: A Life Transformed

We often do not know the burdens people carry, the silent struggles hidden behind their smiles. However, a single word of comfort, spoken in love and guided by the Holy Spirit, can change the trajectory of a person's life. I experienced this first-hand at a seemingly ordinary event, a child's birthday party, where a simple conversation became the turning point in a woman's life.

It was the birthday celebration of a seven-year-old child. The atmosphere was filled with laughter, joy, and the excited chatter of children playing. Amidst the festivities, I found myself in conversation with another parent, a woman who appeared cheerful on the surface but whose eyes betrayed deep sorrow. As we spoke, I felt the Holy Spirit prompting me to share words of encouragement and hope.

She slowly opened up, revealing her struggles: brokenness, despair, and a separation from her husband. She felt lost, without purpose, and was battling overwhelming feelings of hopelessness. In that moment, I did not offer my own wisdom but allowed the Holy Spirit to guide my words. I assured her of God's love, His ability to heal, and His power to restore. I invited her to church and shared scriptures and personal testimonies of God's faithfulness, reminding her that she was not alone and that He had a divine plan for her life.

She later accepted Jesus Christ as her personal Saviour and, in time, decided to be baptized. When the day of her baptism arrived, she asked me to pray for her during the service. It was a deeply moving experience to witness her public declaration of faith.

During the baptismal service at church, she shared her testimony with the congregation, crediting everything that had unfolded to a single conversation we had at her child's birthday party. She spoke about how that one encounter; though seemingly insignificant at the time was, in fact, a divine appointment that totally transformed her life. How could I have possibly known? That moment truly marked the beginning of a journey for her from despair to hope!

But the miracle did not end there. After surrendering her life to Christ, she experienced a new found peace and joy. This transformation led to reconciliation with her husband, from whom she had been separated. He too was deeply moved by the change in her life. A few weeks later, he also accepted Christ, was baptized, and together they renewed their wedding vows, rededicating their marriage to God.

This experience powerfully affirmed that words, when guided by the Holy Spirit, carry immense authority. As Proverbs 18:21 (ESV) declares, "Death and life are in the power of the tongue, and those who love it will eat its fruit." A single act of obedience; speaking life into someone's darkness, can ignite a ripple effect of healing, restoration, and redemption.

Proverbs 15:23 (NIV) reminds us that, "A person finds joy in giving an apt reply, and how good is a timely word!"

This verse emphasises the power of a well-spoken word, aligning with the idea that one conversation or word of comfort can have a significant impact on someone's life and faith journey.

In times of hardship, God offers us His comfort, guiding and supporting us through our struggles. This divine comfort isn't just for our own peace; it is also meant to equip us to comfort others who are facing their own challenges. As we receive God's grace and solace, we are called to share that same comfort with those in need, extending the same compassion we have been shown.

This principle is beautifully expressed in 2 Corinthians 1:4 (NIV), which states, "Who comforts us in all our troubles, so that we can comfort those in any trouble with the comfort we ourselves receive from God."

To Care and So to Teach

Over my decades in education, from kindergarten/reception, primary, junior high, secondary, to university, I have witnessed the transformative power of empathy. I have lectured at university, trained teachers on the Master's Postgraduate Diploma in Education Programme (PGDE), mentored colleagues, and walked alongside students through their struggles and triumphs in Jamaica, The Cayman Islands and the United Kingdom.

Every lesson I impart and every interaction I engage in is infused with the spirit of that pivotal moment in my youth, the understanding that one kind word, one compassionate act, can change a life forever. Galatians 6:9 (NIV) urges us, "Let us not grow weary in doing good, for at the proper time we will reap a harvest if we do not give up." This scripture encapsulates my journey, as every seed of kindness sown has yielded fruit beyond what I could have imagined.

As I honour my beloved parents, Mrs. Thelma and the late Mr. Lamech O'Connor, I am profoundly grateful for the sacrifices they made to give us opportunities they never had. Although their formal education ended at the primary level, their unwavering determination, boundless love, and relentless commitment to their children's future paved the way to success for all of us.

Through countless hardships, they ensured that we had the education and foundation to build better lives. Their sacrifices bore fruit: five of their children embraced the noble calling of teaching, one in Pharmacy, while two dedicated themselves to the nursing profession, in Mental Health (MA) and Midwifery.

The lives of my parents were a testament to Proverbs 22:6 (NIV): "Train up a child in the way he should go, and when he is old he will not depart from it." Today, I stand on the solid ground they built with their perseverance, and I honour them with the deepest gratitude in my heart.

Lost Hope Reclaimed after Despair

Embracing life after secondary school was a journey fraught with challenges, tough decisions, and even moments of deep self-doubt. The weight of choosing a career path and defining my personal direction loomed over me, shaped heavily by my early formation. Hard domestic work on our farm had built resilience in me, but it also left me physically and mentally exhausted at a critical juncture, my GCSE exams.

With little preparation, I fell short of the required exam passes needed for college entry. Yet, by sheer grace, after six months working as a Junior Accounting Clerk at the Jamaica Information Service (JIS), I was granted acceptance at The Mico Teachers' College (Now Mico University), on the condition that I complete an additional GCSE subject (Mathematics), over the next three years.

Despite the daunting nature of college work, I pressed on. In my first year, I defied expectations and passed the additional Math GCSE that was required of me! That freed me up to focus on my College work. With grit, determination, and fervent prayer, I overcame my fears, took a leap of faith and accomplished this. This was no easy feat. I was drained, tired, and stretched up to my limits; yet I moved forward, trusting God every step of the way.

During my time at College, I not only did my Grade 3 Football Referee's licence but also the Royal Schools of Music Theory Grades 3 and 5 and Pianoforte Grades 4 and 6, which mean practising hours daily.

Adjusting to the rigors of academic life was an extreme challenge. The workload was relentless, and balancing it with extracurricular activities including singing on the College Male Voice and Combined Choirs at all major events including graduations demanded a significant portion of my time. This did not include going back to the village termly and participating in the youth concerts and church programmes, including preaching on youth Sundays, playing the guitar and so on.

Still, I persevered, refusing to buckle under the weight of it all. By the time I graduated from Mico Teachers' College in 1985, assessed by the Joint Board of Teacher Education – University of the West Indies, I was just a grade below distinction. Praise God!

Life After Teachers' College

Determined to keep pushing forward, I taught for four years while simultaneously embarking on a BA in Management Studies at the University of the West Indies on a part time basis. This took immense faith, but the confidence I gained from my teacher training propelled me. I had not failed a single course in Teachers' College, and that assurance carried me through.

University was gruelling. Studying part-time meant long nights at the library, then journeying home via two buses, sometimes walking part of the way. Still, I successfully completed in my first two years: Politics, Economics, Sociology, Accounting 1, Commercial Law and Organisational Theory and Behaviour (OTB).

Then, the unexpected happened. In preparation for years three and four, I took leave from work, securing my place for full-time study, only to discover that the Housing Officer had forgotten to secure my room at the halls of residence. Suddenly, I was homeless. To make matters worse, I narrowly failed Mathematics and Statistics, a prerequisite for advancing to Part 2 of my degree, BSC in Management Studies.

The weight of deprivation and isolation was crushing. It was my first and only failure since my GCSE, a brutal and devastating setback. Faced with the options of changing my course or taking a leave of absence, I found myself unable to think clearly and involuntarily stepped away from my studies, after a few meetings with course directors.

I had to contemplate and strategise my way forward. After a few months of being homeless and destitute, I got a job as a Line manager in a Garment Factory, where I stayed for six months before obtaining a teaching post in a Primary school as a Music teacher. These were good days!

Under the expert guidance of the late Mrs Sewell, I not only trained and conducted the school choir for TV programmes like RJR's Colgate Cavity Fighters' Club, Music Corner and others, but also had Graduation performances with my primary school choir. The highlight for me then was preparing for and conducting, along with Mrs Sewell, my school's mass choir to perform 'Jamaica Land of Beauty' at the swearing-in ceremony at Jamaica House for former Prime Minister Hon P. J. Paterson in 1991.

After 4 wonderful years at this primary school, I then accepted a teaching post in the Cayman Islands, where I spent six years educating students in a Christian school, while also serving as a full-time youth minister in the last three years.

During this period, I expanded my horizons, producing and presenting my own four-hour radio program, "Times of Refreshing" on ICCI FM101.1 from 1995-2001; preaching, doing painting and construction work, and even teaching piano lessons. Yet, despite these achievements, I was in no place to consider returning to my studies.

Relocating to England – A new Chapter

Then, in July 2001, I relocated to England, my birth country, with my wife, a turning point in my life. The challenges of adjusting to a new country, carving out a life here, and rebuilding from scratch could fill another book entirely. But one thing was clear: I began to reflect deeply on all I had lost or surrendered in despair. A lingering thought persisted: I was meant to achieve much more. There was greatness within me. I had not yet fulfilled my potential.

There's a saying: "The sweetest revenge is massive success." With a vengeance, I resolved to reclaim everything I had lost. This decision was terrifying. I was stepping back into academia after more than 15 years; my last experience ending in failure. It demanded everything I had left in me. As always, I sought God's direction, prayed fervently, and then moved forward. But the enormity of the challenge must not be underestimated.

Not only was I adjusting to a new culture and system, but I was also managing intense responsibilities: working full-time as a teacher responsible for 720 students per fortnight, enduring gruelling travel times, stacking shelves on weekends and holidays at the local supermarket, doing janitorial work, running our entrepreneurial venture, speaking in ten churches when so invited, facilitating youth seminars and playing bass guitar in my church Praise and Worship band. Against this backdrop, I recommenced my academic journey.

This is only part of my story; a snapshot in time. A testament to faith, perseverance, and the unwavering belief that setbacks do not define us, our response to them does. I went back, I fought, and I reclaimed what I sincerely believed I was capable of achieving.

Do not Let Your Past Define You!

If you've ever felt lost or doubted your own worth, know that you can rise again. You have the power to reclaim what was lost, restore hope after despair, and step into the greatness that has always been within you.

Life's journey frequently takes us through challenges and hardships before guiding us to moments of triumph. My own story is a testament to God's unwavering faithfulness and the power of perseverance. Although I achieved only average GCSE results in 1981 due to circumstances outlined in this book, I refused to let my past define me or dictate my future. I was determined to take back all that I lost and reclaimed hope after my despair.

I must reiterate what I said in my introduction: While this narrative has centred largely on academic restoration, it would be incomplete to overlook the broader, more intricate dimensions of true renewal. Restoration is not confined to the intellect alone; it reaches into the emotional, spiritual, relational, financial and deeply personal aspects of our lives. The path to wholeness calls us to engage with the full complexity of our experiences; not in pursuit of perfection, but in a courageous reclaiming of hope.

It is through this holistic journey, often forged in the aftermath of adversity and 'the school of hard knocks' that we begin to rediscover meaning, rebuild purpose, and emerge with a more integrated sense of self, far beyond the academic sphere.

The qualifications shared throughout this work are not presented as a measure of complete or ultimate success in a narrow or conventional sense. Rather, they are offered as a testament to the possibility of healing and forward movement. They serve not to elevate academic achievement as the only form of success, but to humbly acknowledge a personal journey marked by resilience, perseverance, and the slow, deliberate work of reclaiming hope after despair.

May these words comfort and remind you, as they have reminded me, that restoration is not only possible it is promised. And it unfolds not only in institutions or accolades, but in the quiet, everyday acts of courage, healing, and hope.

Through God's grace and a determined spirit, I pursued academic excellence and personal growth, ultimately by His grace, mercy and divine favour earning in Jamaica a Diploma in Teaching (1985) and in the United Kingdom:

- Personal Social Health Education (PSHE) Certification (2004)
- Qualified Teacher Status (QTS), (2008)
- BA in Education (Hons) First Class (2008)
- MA in Leadership and Management with Distinction (2011)
- Doctorate in Education – Christianity and Faith in Education (2018)

The Cost of a Doctorate: A Journey of Faith, Endurance, and Sacrifice

Reflecting on the last 6 months in 2017 of my doctoral journey, I sometimes shudder at the sheer challenge of balancing intense academic demands with full-time work, part-time ministry, and entrepreneurial pursuit. Managing all my responsibilities earlier mentioned, while simultaneously drafting and revising thesis chapters, obtaining ethical approvals, and preparing for submission, was nothing short of fervently demanding and extremely challenging.

The process culminated in the submission of my final thesis to external examiners in December 2017, followed by both mock and real thesis defences (Viva Voce), January and March 2018 respectively. Even after a successful defence, amendments were required. Though I was given six months to complete them, I managed to finish in just two.

Immediately afterward, in April 2018, I travelled to Jamaica to pay tribute and serve as a pallbearer at my mother-in-law's funeral. This, however, is only part of the story. The journey was far more complex than just an intellectual challenge, it demanded resilience, sacrifice, and faith. Like David and his men, it is not only about reclaiming hope after despair, but the character refinement through the process,

To God be the glory!

A Tribute from Professor TC (Panel Chairman)

No wonder in a tribute for my doctoral thanksgiving celebration Professor TC writes:

> *Phillip O'Connor was a key member of the Jubilee "Christianity and Education" cohort of the Professional Doctorate programme established in 2012 at Christ Church to mark the University's 50th anniversary. Christ Church was founded by the Church of England to train teachers for church schools. It seemed a fitting gesture to mark the Jubilee with a cohort of doctoral students focusing on the Christian contribution to education.*

> *Phillip's thesis tackled one of the most important and challenging topics facing Christian PSHE teachers, namely how do they reconcile their personal Christian commitment with the controversial nature of the subject matter they teach. His extensive empirical study was a mammoth undertaking and was conducted with rigour and resilience.*

Phillip's external examiner was one of the leading professors in the area and the final award of the degree was earned under rigorous interrogation. It is a tribute to Phillip that he has succeeded at the highest level of academia whilst holding down a teaching post. There are few people who manage to do that. And it is also a tribute to Rhona who has supported him on his long academic journey. For me one of the joys of my time at Christ Church has been sharing a journey with Phillip.

Furthermore, for my Reviews leading to my Viva voce, my supervisors wrote:

'Phillip's 7 chapters contain significant signs that it could potentially be a very strong thesis and we are delighted to see how much his thinking and work have developed. The interviews have produced very interesting and important data of a kind that addresses the purpose of the Christianity and education doctoral cohort.' (Prof. BB - First Supervisor's comments after Final review)

'Phillip submitted a significant piece of work to the Panel. The work demonstrates that he has made good progress in his analysis and more importantly, his understanding of some really interesting and important issues.' (Prof. LR – Second Supervisor)

Phillip is to be congratulated on producing a substantial draft of his thesis. He has worked incredibly hard on his empirical research, his engagement with the literature and his writing style has made massive improvement since his last review.

Particularly impressive is his data collection he has undertaken with the teachers. His analysis of that lays bare the challenges that they experienced in seeking to integrate their personal Christian convictions with the requirements of teaching PSHE.

The potential contribution of this thesis lies in the discussion of the strategies that teachers adopted. Potentially, this could be a significant contribution to an important topic. ***Phillip's thesis epitomises the sort of work we had hoped would emerge from the Jubilee Cohort'*** *(Prof TC – Final Review Panel Chairman)*

Following the successful defence of my thesis, my External examiners agreed that:

"The thesis was well-written, thoughtful and original, on a topic of some significance to the teaching profession – and beyond - about the particular experiences of teachers of PSHE who have strong Christian beliefs and convictions, which have various origins and are in transition, and which sometimes present these teachers with dilemmas in their working lives.

They adopt a range of strategies for resolution or compromise. It was evident that great care had been taken in the writing of the thesis, which was clear in its presentation of the literature, methodology and, to a large extent, the data and conclusions from the research.

"Phillip was thoughtful and articulate throughout the viva. His ability to pinpoint specific arguments and to refer the Examiners to precise page numbers in his thesis was most impressive and indicated that he was extremely well rehearsed in the discussion of his work and prepared for its defence."

My examiners, Professor J.S. (External) and Professor S.P. (Internal), concurred that the study met the standards required for a Doctoral degree and extended their commendations and congratulations to Phillip for his work.

Their feedback and comments acknowledge the extensive effort, dedication, perseverance, and personal sacrifices I invested over the course of approximately five and a half years. The journey, marked by rigorous academic demands and moments of profound isolation, has been one of resilience and determination, even in the face of significant personal challenges. As John Newton aptly expressed it:

'Through many dangers, toils and snares, we have already come, Tis grace that brought me home thus far and grace will lead me home!' " (Amazing Grace, 1772).

Inspired by David's Account at Ziglag

In every challenge, my heart is filled with gratitude for the strength I've found in God's word. Psalm 28:7 (NIV) reassures me: "The Lord is my strength and my shield; my heart trusts in Him, and He helps me." Even in times of struggle and uncertainty, I clung to the comforting promise of Isaiah 41:10 (NIV): "So do not fear, for I am with you; do not be dismayed, for I am your God. I will strengthen you and help you; I will uphold you with my righteous right hand."

These verses have been my foundation, reminding me that true success is not just about personal effort but about trusting in God's guidance and provision. Looking back, I see how His strength carried me through difficulties, shaping my resilience and leading me to this moment of achievement.

Ending Where it all Began

At the height of my responsibilities as Head Boy, I found myself overworked overwhelmed by domestic chores that stretched me probably to my limits. The weight of these responsibilities bore heavily on my academic performance in Year 11 (1980), leaving me exhausted and struggling to keep up. It was a defining period of my life, where adversity threatened to derail my ambitions, but it was also the furnace in which resilience, faith, and determination were forged.

Reflecting on my journey, I acknowledge the tremendous pain and sacrifice that accompanied those moments of hardship. It took unwavering faith and an unrelenting spirit to press forward despite the odds. The struggles I faced were not just academic but deeply personal, moments of doubt, exhaustion, and the temptation to surrender to despair. Yet, through it all, I persevered.

Much like David at Ziklag, I encountered a season of disappointment, distress and despair. David, upon returning to find his home burned and his people taken captive, wept until he had no strength left. However, rather than allowing grief to consume him, he sought strength in the Lord and took decisive action to reclaim what was lost.

His story, in certain aspects, strongly resonates with mine. While the extent of David's devastation and initial loss is not entirely comparable to my own, there are similarities. Some parallels can be observed, offering valuable lessons.

I know what it's like to feel completely shattered, overwhelmed by loss and uncertainty. But rather than letting despair consume me, I leaned into my faith, finding strength in the midst of hardships. I refused to let my struggles define me, and with unwavering determination, I pressed on, rediscovering hope where there once was none. How about you?

Strength Made Perfect in Weakness

In moments of struggle, it is easy to believe that we are alone, that the weight of our burdens is ours to bear alone. However, like David, I discovered that in my weakest moments, God's strength was made perfect.

By choosing faith over fear, by refusing to be defined by setbacks, I tapped into an unshakable power that propelled me forward. The journey from struggle to success was neither smooth nor easy, it demanded resilience, courage, and an unwavering belief in a better future.

Today, as I stand on the other side of those trials, I recognise the magnitude of what has been achieved. The success I now enjoy is not merely the result of hard work but also of faith, perseverance, and an unyielding resolve to overcome. Every painful sacrifice, every tear shed, and every ounce of strength summoned in those dark moments has led to this triumph.

My story is a testament to the power of resilience, a reminder that even in our lowest moments, restoration and success are within reach for those who dare to believe, persist, and reclaim what was once lost...hope after and over despair!

No setback, no loss, no hardship is permanent if we lean into the promises of God. Trust that He is with you, guiding you through the darkness and leading you into restoration. Like David, you have the ability to rise again, stronger and more resilient than before. Keep pressing on, knowing that your victory is on the other side of your faith and persistence.

Sincere Gratitude and Grateful Thanks

I am deeply thankful, knowing that God's hand has guided me, turning every trial into a testimony of His faithfulness.

I want to express my deepest and most sincere gratitude to all who have shaped me into the person I am today. Your love, guidance, support, and wisdom have been invaluable in my faith journey. I am deeply grateful for your unwavering love, guidance, and sacrifices which have helped shaped my values and given me the strength to pursue my dreams.

My wife and children, colleagues, employers, my parents and siblings, university professors and other networks. Thanks also to the community of faith which continues to be a constant source of encouragement, instilling in me resilience, hope, and a sense of purpose.

I am also immensely thankful for my friends and extended family, whose support, laughter, and companionship have enriched my journey, making even the toughest challenges more bearable. To my school teachers at all levels, church family from youth, colleagues, mentors, and professional network, I extend my heartfelt appreciation for your wisdom, collaboration, and belief in my abilities. Each of you has played an invaluable role in my growth and success, and I am forever grateful for your presence in my life.

As the process of life continues, I remain committed to seeking God's will and direction, striving to fulfil His purpose for my life. Through every season, I have learned that gratitude and humility open the heart to greater blessings, and I hold onto the words of Scripture: "I thank my God upon every remembrance of you." (Philippians 1:3, KJV).

Life has been a journey of faith, perseverance, and purpose. It is my hope that at the end of life's journey, like the Apostle Paul I too, with confidence, can say: "I have fought a good fight, I have finished my course, I have kept the faith." (2 Timothy 4:7,KJV).

May God continue to lead and direct my path as I press on toward His divine purpose.

Final Word to Motivate, Inspire, Challenge, Encourage & Empower

If you're feeling discouraged or believe that your past failures define your future, let my journey be a reminder; God is not finished with you yet. Consider Jabez, who though born in pain and considered dishonourable, cried out to God in 1 Chronicles 4:10 (NIV): "Oh, that you would bless me and enlarge my territory! Let your hand be with me, and keep me from harm so that I will be free from pain." And God granted his request.

No matter where you are today, your story is still being written. Keep believing, keep striving, and trust that the best is yet to come. Be encouraged. Through faith, perseverance, and God's guidance, lost hope can be restored, and despair can be transformed into triumph, as you make an overwhelming comeback.

Conclusion

———————— 99 ————————

As you turn the final pages of this book, I want you to know that your journey is not over. This is not the end; it is a new beginning. Whatever you have lost: hope, joy, purpose, peace, relationship, influences, reputation, finances, career, know that it is not gone forever. You can take it back. You have the power to reclaim it all: your strength, your vision, your faith, and your future. As the saying goes, it's not about how you start, but how you finish. So finish strong!

The imagery of the potter and the clay is a profound biblical metaphor that illustrates God's sovereign role in shaping and reshaping lives. This concept is vividly captured in Jeremiah 18:4 (KJV): "And the vessel that he made of clay was marred in the hand of the potter: so he made it again another vessel, as seemed good to the potter to make it."

This scripture speaks to the reality of transformation, where imperfections, failures, and brokenness do not render a person useless but rather position them for renewal under divine craftsmanship.

In life, there are seasons of crushing, moulding, and reshaping, moments that may require reskilling, retraining, and even finding new associations. Just like the clay on the potter's spinning wheel, we may feel the pressure of circumstances, the unsettling motion of change, or even the discomfort of being broken down to be remade.

However, what remains constant is the presence of the Potter. His hands never leave the clay; His foot never lifts from the pedal controlling the spin. This means that no flaw, mistake, or deficiency can intimidate the Potter, and no situation we face is beyond His knowledge or ability to transform.

The process of reformation under the Potter's hands is not a sign of abandonment but of intention. Isaiah 64:8 (KJV) affirms this by saying, "But now, O Lord, thou art our father; we are the clay, and thou our potter; and we all are the work of thy hand." This acknowledgment reinforces that every reshaping is for a greater purpose. Even when we feel displaced or uncertain about the next step, we can trust that God is refashioning, rebranding, and renewing us for a higher calling.

Just as clay submits to the Potter's hands, we, too, must embrace the seasons of transformation with faith. There will be times when the reshaping process feels uncomfortable, when old structures are dismantled, and when our journey requires us to learn new skills or build fresh connections. Yet, in the end, the result is a vessel made anew, one that is stronger, more refined, and prepared for its intended use.

The promise remains: after the spinning, shaping, and even crushing, we are still in the Potter's hands. The journey is not one of destruction but of construction and restoration. As we yield to the process, we will experience the fullness of God's renewal being rekindled in spirit, revived in purpose, and restored in vision, all under the guidance of the divine Potter.

Fear Not

Life's struggles do not define you; your response to them does. We are reminded that, "You have been trapped by what you said, ensnared by the words of your mouth." (Proverbs 6:2, NIV). You have been equipped with everything you need to rise again, to rebuild, to press forward with courage and determination.

As Isaiah 41:10 (NIV) reminds us, "So do not fear, for I am with you; do not be dismayed, for I am your God. I will strengthen you and help you; I will uphold you with my righteous right hand." You are not alone in this battle. God walks beside you, strengthening you for every challenge ahead.

I challenge you today: do not settle for a life less than what you were created for. Take hold of your calling. Galatians 6:9 (NIV) encourages us, "Let us not become weary in doing good, for at the proper time we will reap a harvest if we do not give up." The path to restoration requires perseverance, but the reward is great. Keep going. Keep believing. Keep reclaiming all that is rightfully yours.

You have a purpose beyond your pain. You have a future beyond your failures. Like the prodigal son who returned home (Luke 15:11-32), you can return to the place of hope, restoration, and wholeness. You are not forgotten, nor are you forsaken. God's grace is sufficient for you, His strength made perfect in your weakness (2 Corinthians 12:9).

A Life Restored – Mephibosheth

Mephibosheth's story for example, is a powerful testament to grace, restoration, and hope after despair. He was the son of Jonathan and the grandson of King Saul, but after his father and grandfather died in battle, he was left crippled as a child and abandoned in Lo-Debar, a desolate place of barrenness and obscurity (2 Samuel 4:4).

For years, Mephibosheth lived in isolation, forsaken and forgotten. However, King David, out of his covenant love for Jonathan, sought him out and brought him to the palace. Instead of judgment or rejection, David restored Mephibosheth's inheritance and granted him a permanent place at the royal table. From that day forward, he was no longer an outcast but sat at the king's table as one of his own sons, waited upon by servants, and treated with honour (2 Samuel 9:1-13).

His journey from forsaken to favoured reflects the transformative power of grace; turning despair into hope and restoring dignity to the broken.

Final Word

Reclaiming hope after despair is never easy. The journey is often filled with invisible battles, grief that lingers, trust that feels shattered, confidence that seems beyond repair. For some, it's the weight of past failures; for others, it's the silence after heartbreak, the slow burn of disappointment, or the crushing blow of unexpected change. Each person's valley looks different, but the struggle is real.

Not all stories have happy endings; not in the way we often imagine. If you're reading this with a heavy heart, with broken pieces scattered at your feet, know this: your story isn't over. And it's okay if it doesn't look like someone else's victory. Sometimes, God doesn't remove the pain or undo the loss. Sometimes, instead, He whispers, "My grace is sufficient for thee, for my strength is made perfect in weakness" (2 Corinthians 12:9, KJV).

You may feel like you're walking through fire or drowning in floods of sorrow, but you are not alone. Isaiah 43:2 (NKJV) reminds us: "When you pass through the waters, I will be with you... when you walk through the fire, you shall not be burned."

Some go through fire. Some through flood; but all of us go through by the blood and the redeeming, sustaining grace of Jesus Christ.

Your journey may not unfold the way you had planned, but that doesn't mean it's off course. God is sovereign. Like the potter in Jeremiah 18:4 (KJV), God can take what feels broken and marred and make it again another vessel, as seemed good to the potter to make it. Success may not look like what you once imagined, but in God's hands, every outcome has purpose.

In my book, *Safely Through on Broken Pieces*, I encourage you to: *"Focus on what you have left, not on what you have lost."* That's not denial, it's a courageous stand. Reclaiming hope after despair is not easy. The valleys we walk are real - valleys filled with silent grief, lingering disappointments, fragile trust, and battles nobody else sees. For some, it's the pain of past failure. For others, it's heartbreak that was never quite healed.

But friend, even here and now, hope is not dead. It's buried deep, waiting to be uncovered. Restoration doesn't always come all at once. It sometimes begins with small steps: reaching out, speaking the truth, daring to believe that healing is still possible. Psalm 147:3 (NIV) declares, "He heals the brokenhearted and binds up their wounds." This is a God who doesn't discard the broken. God rebuilds them.

You may be clinging to life by a thread, or drifting ashore on broken pieces of what used to be. Still, you're here. You've survived. And that, in itself, is a miracle. Just as those in Acts 27:44 made it safely to land on shattered pieces of their ship, you too can make it; not necessarily untouched, but preserved. Not unharmed, but redeemed.

So keep showing up. Keep breathing. Keep believing. Remember, "Weeping may endure for a night, but joy comes in the morning"

(Psalm 30:5, NKJV). Let that promise guide you; not to rush your pain, but to trust your process and above all else, trust God's heart even when you cannot trace his hand. Reclamation should not be understood as a singular moment of triumph, but rather as a gradual and sacred process of restoring wholeness, marked by intentional and grace-filled progression over time.

Be gentle with yourself. You don't have to have it all together to be in God's will. You just have to be willing. Let the Potter do His work. He's not finished with you yet.

Reclaim your hope. Take back your joy. Walk boldly in your purpose. The race is not over; the best is yet to come; Your best days are ahead of you!

This is the powerful truth I've learned from David and his men at Ziklag. Although their city was burnt to the ground and everything seemed lost, through God's strength, they rose, pursued, and recovered all.

Now, go take it back: Reclaim your hope after despair.

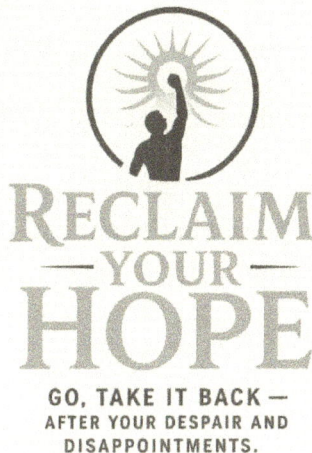

RECLAIM
—YOUR—
HOPE
GO, TAKE IT BACK —
AFTER YOUR DESPAIR AND
DISAPPOINTMENTS.

Psalm 61 (NLT)

———— 99 ————

A Psalm of David

1 O God, listen to my cry!   Hear my prayer!

2 From the ends of the earth,   I cry to you for help when my heart is overwhelmed.   Lead me to the towering rock of safety,

3 For you are my safe refuge,   a fortress where my enemies cannot reach me.

4 Let me live forever in your sanctuary,   safe beneath the shelter of your wings!

5 For you have heard my vows, O God.   You have given me an inheritance reserved for those who fear your name.

6 Add many years to the life of the king!   May his years span the generations!

7 May he reign under God's protection forever. May your unfailing love and faithfulness watch over him.

8 Then I will sing praises to your name forever   as I fulfil my vows each day.

References

———— 99 ————

Counselling Directory (2024) *Men and mental health*. Available at: https://www.counselling-directory.org.uk/men.html (Accessed: 1 July 2025).

Kübler-Ross, E., 1969. *On Death and Dying*. New York: Macmillan.

Office for National Statistics (2023) *Suicides in England and Wales: 2022 registrations*. Available at: https://www.ons.gov.uk/peoplepopulationandcommunity/birthsde athsandmarriages/deaths/bulletins/suicidesintheunitedkingdom/20 22registrations (Accessed: 1 July 2025).

Office for National Statistics. (2024, August 29). *Suicides in England and Wales: 2023 registrations*. Retrieved from Office for National Statistics website.

Samaritans (2023) *Socioeconomic disadvantage and suicidal behaviour: Position statement*. [online] Available at: https://www.samaritans.org/about-samaritans/research-policy/socioeconomic-disadvantage-suicide/ [Accessed 1 Jul. 2025].

The Guardian. (2024, August 29). *Suicide rates in England and Wales reach highest level since 1999*. The Guardian.

Appendix

———— 99 ————

Dear Dr. O'Connor,

I hope this message finds you well. My name is X, and I had the privilege of being in your Personal Social Health Education (PSHE) class between 2016 and 2019.

While it's been a few years, **I wanted to reach out personally and express my gratitude for the profound impact you had on my educational journey.** You may not recall me, but I remember our interactions vividly.

During my time at school, I struggled with behaviour and focus in my classes, affecting my grades and potentially jeopardizing my path to further education. **I distinctly remember a moment when my misbehaviour led to a conversation with you,** where you warned me about the consequences of my choices and advised me to prioritize my academic development.

At the time, I may not have fully grasped the significance of your words, but looking back, **I can confidently say that it was a turning point for me. Your guidance made me realize the privilege of education and instilled in me a commitment to take it seriously.**

After leaving (school) in 2019, I completed my GCSEs and A levels, culminating in my graduation summer 2023. I am thrilled to share that I am currently in the second year of a degree in Medicine at the University of X (UK), with aspirations of becoming a medical doctor. If someone had told me in year 9 that this would be my path, I wouldn't have believed them. **I attribute the start of my academic turnaround to that one lunchtime detention and your impactful advice.**

I want to express my sincere gratitude, Dr. O'Connor, for taking the time to guide me and redirect me from a potentially destructive path. **I genuinely believe I wouldn't be the person I am today without that conversation.** Your dedication to educating and shaping the youth has left a lasting impression on me.

This particular quote and wise-saying of yours has served me well through the years 'Whenever a task is once begun, never leave it 'till it's done, be it little, great or small, do it well or not at all (but not at all is not an option)'. I find that I can apply this to almost every aspect of life and I will certainly never forget it!

I wish you all the best in your future endeavours and once again, **thank you for being an influential part of my journey.**

Warm regards,

(Past Student)

www.ingramcontent.com/pod-product-compliance
Lightning Source LLC
LaVergne TN
LVHW011348080426
835511LV00005B/193